Steve & y

*Now that you're both
back in the bleachers, I
hope you might enjoy this.*

CAESAR'S WIFE

Dave

David A. Williams

CAESAR'S WIFE

The College President's Spouse/Partner:

Minister without Portfolio or the President's Conscience

David A. Williams

Railroad Street Press
St. Johnsbury, Vermont

LIBRARY OF CONGRESS
CATALOGING-IN-PUBLICATION DATA

Williams, David A.

Caesar's Wife / David A. Williams.

ISBN 9781936711307

Railroad Street Press
394 Railroad St., Suite 2
St. Johnsbury, Vermont
www.railroadstreepress.com

DISCLAIMER

Portions of the contents of this book relate to legal concepts. The inclusion of this type of material is intended for informational and educational purposes only. It is _not offered as, nor is it intended to be taken or used as, legal advice_. The laws of many jurisdictions vary significantly. If legal advice is desired, it should be obtained from a competent lawyer licensed to practice (and practicing) in the particular jurisdiction involved. The author specifically disclaims any guarantee or warranty (expresses or implied) relating to the local or general accuracy or usability of any of the contents of this book for legal purposes; and further, the author does not represent that legal materials included in this book are current or complete. Nothing in this book shall be construed to create an attorney/client relationship between the author and any other person.

University Park

STUDENT'S WAY

BOARD WAY

CREATIVITY

COMPENSATION

President's
Office

President's
House

ALUMNI

FACULTY ROAD

ADMINISTRATION
ALLEY

STAFF STREET

ACKNOWLEDGMENTS

A book discussing the role of and reason for college presidents' spouse/partners could not be written absent the existence of college presidents. Without President (now emerita) Peggy Williams, I would be writing something else—or nothing at all. Although I taught college courses as an adjunct before meeting Peggy, my seat at the higher education concert hall, then, was pretty far back in the upper balcony. As her higher education involvement graduated from community college academic counselor to community college regional director to state college system director to independent college dean to public college president to independent college president, my seat moved ever closer to the stage and more toward the center. Eventually, as the president's spouse, I enjoyed center, orchestra seats at most college venues (literally and metaphorically).

From those seats, a person's sense of importance to the college can quickly expand to unwarranted proportions. Happily, the woman seated next to me at these venues was someone who preferred to be called, not "Dr./President Margaret Ryan Williams," but rather "Peggy." She unaccountably knew not only the names of hundreds (or perhaps thousands) of college folks, but also the names of spouses, children, and pets of these same folks. In conversation with someone whom I had never met she could unerringly inquire about the outcome of "Rebecca's" middle school soccer tournament and the state of health of "Rebecca's" dog, "Bruno." As members of the college community opened to her, she opened all the doors and windows of the college to me. She enabled me to learn servant leadership and to share in the intangible rewards of membership in the higher education community. My love and respect for her and my gratitude to her are boundless.

I also thank all of the participants in AASCU and CIC spouse sessions who provided me with the lion's share of the material for this book. In particular I thank those who shared their disappointments and their inability to understand apparently hostile and/or disrespectful attitudes of the college communities they sought to serve. I believe these unhappy and benighted spouses represent a majority of presently serving presidential spouses. They deserve to be better treated. It is the responsibility of boards of trustees to see to it that they are better treated—for the sake of both the spouses and the colleges.

I am grateful for the ongoing support and encouragement of my "readers" and "rooters." The readers sacrificed much time and energy providing me with invaluable criticism. These folks included Judith Block McLaughlin, Ed.D.; Ralph L. MacDonald, Jr.; Stan Carpenter, J.D.; Margie Arnold, Ph.D.; Emily Manus, MFA, MSW; Dianne Lynch, Ph.D.; Susan

Scanlon, J.D./M.B.A.; Wrexie Bardaglio, Charles I. Bunting, Ed.D and Alan Boye. The "rooters" included the innumerable folks who induced a pang of guilt in my heart every time they inquired, "How's the book coming?" Now I can say with confidence, "It's done!"

I have noticed over the years that people who attended college draw most of their lifelong friends from their college contemporaries and more particularly from those with whom they lived in college. Somewhat more surprisingly, folks with whom one lived, but did not have a particularly close relationship can emerge decades later as concerned and helpful friends. I have been blessed with just such a serendipitous event—renewing my acquaintance with Nick Goodhue, the editor of this text. I had not seen Nick for almost fifty years, but at a social event in Williamstown, Massachusetts, we reintroduced ourselves. Nick had retired as an editor. Recalling him as a studious and serious fellow, I inquired if he would take on editing this manuscript. *Almost* without hesitation, he agreed. His work with me has been very thorough, occasionally embarrassing, and extremely welcome.

I offer special thanks to Jane Lavery for developing the cover art concept for this book. She captured well the hope beyond the "ivied walls and spiked gates".

Finally, Ralph L. MacDonald, Jr., was an undergraduate roommate, an aspiring (albeit challenged) writer, and a great critic. At my request he read almost every draft of this work, never missing an opportunity to delete an unnecessary comma or to inquire (or better, demand), "Who do you want to read this thing?" I am very thankful for all of that.

CAESAR'S WIFE

CONTENTS

Preface   1

Introduction   7

Chapter 1: "I Get No Respect" in which Jean Kemeny, wife of the then president of Dartmouth, reveals the two contrary states of her being: the confident, self-assured "co-president" of Dartmouth and the disrespected, "volunteered" wife of President John Kemeny. In doing so, she presents a very clear picture of the institutional forces that create the unhappiness which consumes so many college presidents' spouses. She then introduces us to the concept of queenliness. 19

Chapter 2: "Everything Old Is New Again . . ." in which three historical examples of the CEO's wife courting and/or experiencing disenchantment with her role as the professional "wife" are described. Distinctions between offensive and defensive queenliness are discussed. 29

Chapter 3: "Why Do They Hate Me?—Turf Wars" in which the territorial imperatives of the college community are described. The difficulties of the president's spouse trying to navigate the various contested "turfs" and the myriad ways in which the spouse can alienate the college's and broader community's sensibilities are discussed. 45

Chapter 4: "And in Your New Job You Will Report to . . ." in which the basic mechanisms of the college president's spouse's disenchantment are described. They include the assumption by the spouse of supervision of staff or control of college moneys when her exercise of the supervision or control is perceived by the college community as usurpation by a person who holds power only by reason of her marriage to the president—not by virtue of her own talents. She is also condemned because she can never be seen as being subject to the same processes by which all the other employees of the college were hired and are being supervised. 77

Chapter 5: "Jobs, Roles, Money . . . Do Not Mix" in which the ambiguity between the spouse having a "role" at the college and having a "job" at the college is examined, as well as the aggravation of campus relations created by changing a spouse's unpaid "role" to a paid "job." 91

Chapter 6: "Truth . . . or Consequences" in which the potential legal and ethical issues attending the traditional ways in which boards of trustees have defined the role/job of the president's spouse (or simply permitted a preexisting definition to continue) expose the college to legal liability and ethical censure.   105

Chapter 7: "Does She? Or Doesn't She? Only the Development Office Knows for Sure" in which the assertion that the president's spouse is, almost always, an invaluable part of the college's development program is questioned.   127

Chapter 8: "The Contract . . . You Do for Me—I Do for You" in which boards of trustees are urged to create policies under which (beginning with the next president) the president's spouse has no responsibilities to the college. The spouse serves as an occasional volunteer to the college and as a private conscience to the president. In doing so, the spouse supports rather than distracts the president and substantially avoids conflicts of interest or public relations problems which arise when the college or broader community views the spouse as an agent of the college.   137

Chapter 9: "She's Only a Volunteer . . . So What's the Problem?" in which major problems which can be caused by long-term spouse/partner volunteers are examined together with corrective policies and practices which boards should consider.   149

Chapter 10: "Where the Boys Are" in which boards of trustees are urged to limit the authority and closely supervise the actions of assertive male spouses of female college presidents.   159

Chapter 11: "Now the Trouble with All This Knowledge I've Got Hold of Is . . . That It's Useless" in which the considerable intelligence and experience of presidential spouses is celebrated in a reminiscence of the life and times of Muriel Beadle (wife of the former president of the University of Chicago). Boards of trustees are urged to consider selecting presidential spouses to serve as board members of non-competing colleges.   169

Conclusion   181

Appendix A Curriculum Vitae of Constance Bumgarner Gee   191

Appendix B   Draft Complaint in the Matter of George Knot and Gerri Knot v. Northeast Southwest College, et al.   198

Appendix C   Draft Complaint in the Matter of Cube Root and Square Root v. Northeast Southwest College, et al.   203

Appendix D University of Vermont Board of Trustees Policy on Presidential Spouse or Partner Services   207

Preface

On the morning of June 24, 2006, Denice Denton, chancellor[1] of the University of California, Santa Cruz, stepped off a terrace on the forty-second floor of an apartment building in San Francisco, California, and plunged to her death.[2] Chancellor Denton was an extraordinarily accomplished person, holding four engineering degrees from MIT. She had served as the first woman dean of an engineering college in America (University of Washington) and had been appointed chancellor of UC Santa Cruz in 2004.[3] She had been in the audience when Lawrence H. Summers (past president of Harvard University and former White House economic advisor to President Barack Obama) made his infamous remarks about women in the

---

[1] "Chancellor" and "president" are used to designate the CEO of a college or university. Both are used depending on the traditions of the particular institution. When discussing college/university CEOs in general, I will use "president." Otherwise I will use the chosen designation used by the particular CEO.

[2] Cecilia M. Vega and Jaxon VanDerbeken, "UC Santa Cruz Chancellor Dies in Suicide Plunge," *San Francisco Chronicle*, June 25, 2006, http://www.sfgate.com/default/article/UC-Santa-Cruz-chancellor-dies-in-suicide-plunge-2494089.php (accessed March 14, 2013).

[3] "Cal Chancellor's Death Likely Suicide," *CBSNews.com*, http://www.cbsnews.com/stories/2006/06/25/national/main1749430.shtml (accessed March 14, 2013).

sciences. Her critical responses to Summers's remarks were widely quoted.[4] Now she was dead.

In the days and weeks which followed Denton's suicide, many of the stresses and strains under which she labored in her relatively short career at UC Santa Cruz came to light. Issues relating to renovations made to the president's house at her behest and her salary as compared with college rank-and-file employees (who had not received an increase for three years) were discussed.

However, the nexus to which most of the criticisms of Denton's administration adhered related to her partner, Gretchen Kalonji. Denton and Kalonji had worked together at the University of Washington. When Denton moved to Santa Cruz, a position was created for Kalonji as the University of California's director of international strategy development. Kalonji did not report to Denton. The position paid Kalonji $192,000 per year. It is likely that she was well qualified for the position, but that was of no moment to Denton's critics.

When it became known that Kalonji was Denton's lesbian partner, rumors began to fly to the effect that a significant portion of the $600,000 spent on renovations to the chancellor's house was for the benefit of Kalonji.

---

[4] "Here was this economist lecturing pompously to this room full of the country's most accomplished scholars on women's issues in science and engineering, and he kept saying things we had refuted in the first half of the day." Scott Jaschik, "Suicide of a Chancellor," *Inside Higher Ed*, June 26, 2006 (quoting the *Boston Globe*),
http://www.insidehighered.com/news/2006/06/26/denton (accessed March 14, 2013).

Denton's relationship with Kalonji became *the* focus of campus and community discussion.

The UC Santa Cruz community could be ugly.

> ". . . students surrounded Denton's car in the parking lot, refusing to let her get out."

> ". . . in the middle of the night, someone thrust a large metal pole through a window in the president's home. Denton was in another room at the time, but had she been in the room where the glass was broken, she could have been seriously injured."

> ". . . Several other times protestors showed up at her door, refusing to leave."[5]

So venomous was the climate surrounding Denton that just three days after her death, an individual identified only as "P. Ickle" (a nom de plume which was at best disrespectful and at worse vulgar) posted a letter to *Inside Higher Ed* excoriating Denton: "This lesbian administrator, in an effort to create her own 'lesbian culture' . . . , created an ad hoc billet for her partner, to the tune of $192,000 annually. Where was Dr. Denton's vaunted need for diversity then?"[6]

What the chair of the Board of Regents of the University of California thought when he heard the news of Denton's death may never be known, but board chairs and members of other colleges and universities must have heaved a collective sigh of relief that "it" had happened "somewhere else."

---

[5] Jaschik, "Suicide of a Chancellor."

[6] Ibid. When it comes to dancing on coffins, P. Ickle has few serious competitors

Although Denton's suicide is an extreme example of a chancellor's/president's response to the superheated criticism of one university community, shortened tenures, early retirements, and decisions to return to the faculty or "spend more time with my family" are other types of presidential responses through which colleges and universities lose good presidents before their time. Presidents and their families are emotionally scarred, often permanently. College reputations are sullied.

Many factors may contribute to a president's failure, but the one factor which arises with distressing frequency and the one with which I am most familiar is the "president's spouse/partner" factor. More often than not, problems with the president's spouse or partner are completely preventable. Responsibility for such prevention efforts rests predominantly with college and university boards of trustees whose relationships with the president's spouse or partner should be legally and ethically sound and grounded in consistent organizational practices.

There is an old saying that to be successful as a public figure, one must be more virtuous "than Caesar's Wife."[7] This phrase applies with special vigor to the wives, partners, and occasionally the husbands of college presidents. For those of us who have experienced that role, the weight of expectations *can* be overwhelming. It *should not* be so. What follows are (1)

---

[7] Although the traditional admonition was that Caesar's wife had to be "above suspicion," the "more virtuous than" language seems to have more current use.

a plea to college trustees, presidents, and their spouses/partners to lighten that load, and (2) some suggestions of ways to do so.

I am happy to report that most of the stories and incidents which I relate here did not happen to me. I will confess those which involved my wife and me. Otherwise, I learned about them from news accounts, from the materials which are quoted below, from meetings where college presidents' spouses let down (or sometimes seemed to tear out) their hair, and from the lore and legend which is everywhere about the higher education community.

I am forever in the debt of those wise boards and search committees which chose my wife, twice, to serve as the president of their respective institutions of higher education. They did so despite my pre-selection declarations that I would exercise loyalty to my wife and help her in any way I could in the execution of her charge, but that I would not serve the college. I stated to the board chair of one of those colleges, "If you're looking for a president's spouse who has no obligations to the college, I'm your man."

To the great credit of both search committees and boards of trustees, they focused on my wife's credentials and abilities—not on what they thought their respective college communities might extract from me (or what these communities believed I would "owe" them) as the president's spouse. In each instance, the college got exactly what it was entitled to: a great president.

INTRODUCTION

"When the press has finished jumping on her husband
And there's entertainment duty to be done,
Oh, take one consideration with another – with another,
A presidential spouse's lot is not a happy one . . . . "

      . . . With apologies to Gilbert and Sullivan

Now hear this. What follows is directed to the eyes, ears, minds, and hearts of college and university trustees. Others may find this material amusing, entertaining, or maddening, but it is to trustees that I speak. Your president's spouse/partner[8] has a role in the good health of your college or university, and I am willing to make a small wager that habit and tradition have made it difficult for your board to appreciate the serious problems which those habits and traditions can create for you. As a presidential spouse with twenty years' experience, I know about these problems and want you to know what they are and what to do about them.

In 1989, shortly after my wife was appointed President of Lyndon State College, the Chancellor of the Vermont State Colleges encouraged her to attend the

---

[8] For brevity I will use "spouse" in lieu of "spouse/partner."

annual conference of the American Association of State Colleges and Universities (AASCU). She, in turn, urged me to attend with her. In the few days I spent at AASCU, I received impressions which have only proved increasingly useful over the twenty-plus years since that event. These impressions arose as the result of my attendance at so-called Spouse Seminars and from my interactions with the spouses of other college presidents.

I came to this meeting with a few, amorphous concepts of what it meant to be the president's spouse. These concepts arose from my knowledge of and friendships with the wives of several Vermont State College presidents and from somewhat vague recollections of the wives of the presidents of my undergraduate college. The mix of these interactions coupled with my preexisting notion of what my role should be, formed the primordial goop from which the ideas for this work grew.

The wife of the first president of my undergraduate college during my passage there was nearly invisible to me. That president presided over the college during my freshman year only. Both he and his wife were quite advanced in age. I do not recall her saying anything of note (for freshmen ears, anyway) and do not recall seeing much of her. She was very much like the Minister's Wife in the materials which follow.

I better recollect the wife of the second president. She appeared frequently at college events, seemed to be having a good time of it, but rarely spoke. I am sure she was much more talkative and engaged with trustees, donors, and alumni. There seemed to be a role for her, a role which she fulfilled with apparent grace and humor.

The two spouses of Vermont State College presidents whom I knew best were lively women who were very much engaged in the college and political communities in which they lived. They held public office on local school boards and participated in volunteer projects in the larger community. They were both very active as social and institutional hostesses.

They also managed to raise children in campus environments (in the 1970s and 1980s) which surely posed special challenges. Their public personas were energetic, optimistic, and humorous. I felt that I knew them reasonably well (and considerably better than I knew the wives of the presidents of my undergraduate college). However, in unguarded moments, both of these very talented and dedicated women voiced concerns about their roles as presidential spouses and some degree of unhappiness about the attitudes which certain members of the college and town communities displayed toward them. Although my awareness of these concerns and unhappiness was pretty much subliminal in the 1970s and 1980s, my AASCU experiences brought that vague awareness into much sharper focus. Later, I heard similar expressions of concern and unhappiness at CIC (Council of Independent Colleges) presidents' spouses' meetings.

My attitudes about my role as the president's spouse were born of simple necessity. My wife had a career which I supported as fully as I could. She earned her master's and doctorate during our marriage. This required her to live away from our home for two and a half years. That was not easy on us, but we got it done. I accompanied her to events related to her pre-presidential employments in higher education and traveled with her to presidential search interviews.

However, I also had a career. I was a lawyer whose practice was largely involved in litigation (some of which involved employer/employee relationships). I held small-town political office and served on nonprofit boards. There was no practical way for me to fulfill the traditional role of the president's spouse—even if that were my wish. I knew what I could and could not do, and made no secret of those limitations to the search committees which interviewed me. Ultimately, this career-mandated circumstance allowed me to look at the institution of the president's spouse through an untraditional set of eyes. I elected not to simply walk away from the role of the president's spouse but rather to study it, experience it, and seek out the stories and feelings of others who shared that role.

In very broad strokes, this is what I have learned to date:

1. There is a pervasive unhappiness among presidential spouses. It is not universal. This unhappiness is expressed most frequently from presidential spouse to presidential spouse and not from spouse to the college community which she[9] seeks to serve. This unhappiness stems from what spouses describe as "overwork," "underappreciation," and "helplessness in the face of institutional demands."

---

[9] I shall use "she" in place of "she/he." Both genders are intended to be included in the word "she." I shall refer to presidents as "he" in place of "he/she." Both genders are included in the word "he."

2. This unhappiness is not new. Examples exist well back into nineteenth-century America (and, I am sure, before). The wives of college presidents, diplomats, politicians, religious leaders, and business executives have all suffered the same kind of unhappiness and for very similar reasons.

3. When a presidential spouse assumes responsibility for any institutional task which has been performed by an employee of the college,[10] or when that spouse seeks to supervise the work of a college employee, or when the spouse acts in a controversial manner which reflects on the college, the potential for hurtful institutional responses arises.

4. Such hurtful institutional responses arise because the president's spouse occupies a unique place in the academy. She did not compete for her job, usually has no job description, is not subject to meaningful supervision, and is, for all practical purposes, immune from discipline or discharge. Further, her service to the college can raise conflicts of interest between the spouse as college employee and the spouse as friend, helpmate, and conscience of the president.

5. Many a president's spouse has come to grief or anger because of the board of directors' unconcern about whether the spouse is serving in a *role* or whether she is holding a *job*. Although many spouses are not really sure which title they

---

[10] "College" includes "university." "Spouse" includes "husband," "wife," and "same-sex partner."

11

deserve, most believe that there is no money in having a role and that there should be money in having a job. There are hazards to both designations. The *role* of the president's spouse has a long history of exploitation of the volunteered spouse. The *job* of president's spouse is more hazardous still because only one person in the universe can qualify for that job. The sole qualification for that job is that she be married to (or partnered with) the president—which qualification has nothing to do with the holder's ability to do anything. As noted above, the job rarely has a meaningful job description and never involves true supervision, accountability, or discipline. This distinguishes the spouse from all other employees of the college and often creates animosity. When the spouse is paid for her job, the potential for animosity grows. Boards can eliminate this problem by adopting and adhering to a simple rule: The next president's spouse shall have no role and no job and no paycheck.

6. Most boards of trustees are either blind to the deleterious effects of the president's spouse being actively involved in the college's affairs or believe that the services which the spouse traditionally performs are fair recompense for the benefits she receives simply because she lives with the president. Such attitudes are not simply suspect—they may have significant legal consequences. In either case, the issues which boards must address are not simply matters of tradition or organization; they are matters of institutional ethics. Since at least the beginning of

the Women's Liberation Movement, sensible people have looked at the job of the presidential spouse and concluded, correctly, that there is a basic unfairness in the college's expecting the spouse to perform many important functions while she is paid nothing for her efforts. Notwithstanding the arguments of those who advocate compensation for presidential spouses, I argue that compensation simply makes a potentially hurtful situation into a truly hurtful one. Spouse compensation also raises the potential for a conflict of interest between the spouse as a college employee and the spouse as the spouse, friend, helpmate, and conscience of the president.

7. The most frequently asserted justification for the involvement of the president's spouse in college affairs is development. Development refers to all those activities undertaken by a college to enhance relationships with potential donors (both individual and corporate). The purpose of these activities is to raise the money that enables the college to provide facilities and programs for its students which it could not provide from tuition (and, if applicable, government funding) alone. It is widely believed that the active and continuing participation of the president's spouse in planning and executing development functions is indispensable to institutional development efforts. How might one measure the impact which spouses have on development performance? One way to measure the "spouse effect" might be to look at the development performance of colleges where a

changeover occurred from a female to a male presidential spouse. I considered this measurement because female spouses are generally much more involved in development activities than are male spouses. Presumably a changeover from female to male spouse should cause a reduction in development efforts and results. Interestingly, my study of available data suggests that both contribution totals and participation percentages seemed to be unaffected by such a changeover. This raises a heretofore unspoken question: Does the participation of the president's spouse in development work really make a difference to the development bottom line? I conclude that it probably does not.

8. The most happy and fulfilled presidential spouses are those who develop and/or continue lives which are not defined by their relationship to the college. They have abiding loyalty to their president/spouses and courtesy toward the colleges which their spouses serve. Although I have heard many spouses speak about a contract between the college and the spouse, the real and important contract at issue is the one between the president and the spouse. The college should be merely an incidental beneficiary of the interspousal contract. By and large, the college benefits substantially from the vibrant participation of the spouse in her relationship with the president. Spouses with this kind of understanding live happier, more fulfilled, and less resented lives—lives which enrich the president

and the college. In doing so, these spouses make the colleges their spouses head better.

9. The fact that a presidential spouse acts "only as a volunteer" does not eliminate the hazards of her acting in a representative capacity. Spouse indiscretions which would be institutionally meaningless if committed by any other college employee's spouse can become embarrassing front-page stories.

10. Since most colleges have traditionally chosen males to serve as their presidents, the spouses have, until recently, been almost universally female. With improvements in gender equity, more married women are becoming college presidents and their male spouses are coming to grips with some of the issues set out above. Roughly 26 percent of college/university presidents are now female. My observations of presidential spouses at AASCU and CIC conferences have led me to conclude that most of male presidential spouses are not actively participating in the day-to-day affairs of the colleges their wives lead. Unfortunately, there are exceptions to this rule. There is a new breed of presidential spouse. What I will call the "new male spouse" is self-confident and assertive and very much involved in the day-to-day operations of the college. The potential for institutional disruption and dislocation which he brings to the campus community is immense. Faced with a new male spouse, boards should communicate clear limitations on his authority and prerogatives and should diligently monitor his activities.

11. Most spouses of college presidents know a great deal about colleges and their operations, missions, and personalities. This is valuable knowledge which should not go to waste. Such knowledge could best be utilized by presidents' spouses serving as trustees of unrelated, noncompeting colleges.

The chapters which follow are intended to set out the predictable problems which presidents, spouses, college employees, board members, and institutions themselves are likely to encounter if they continue the practice of anticipating that the president's spouse will act as a professional volunteer (compensated or uncompensated) to the college. They are likewise intended to propose models for all of the affected college constituencies and presidential spouses to follow so that the spouse, the college, and the college's employees are better served and happier.

What follow are pleas and a warning to boards, in particular, to reform their views of the proper role of the president's spouse by eliminating all *institutional* expectations for that spouse. Although the bold spouse can start the reformation process, it is more fairly in the bailiwick of the board to initiate that process. Once begun, the board, the president, the spouse, and the college community must be continually reminded that the spouse's first and only loyalty is to the president—not to the college.

Marguerite Walker Corbally surveyed college presidents' spouses in 1975 in an attempt to assess how a wide sample of spouses felt about their roles. One unnamed respondent said, "Presidents' spouses are individuals with hopes, aspirations, and often careers of their own. They should have the freedom to choose. *Boards of Trustees and selection committees should arrive at their choice of president without regard to marital status of candidates or the professions of their spouses. It may be a long time coming, but I predict the role of the president's wife will go the way of the dinosaur.*"[11] (Emphasis added.)

Traditionally, the spouses of college presidents have played out their roles in the capacity of ministers without portfolio. In a parliamentary form of government, this minister is assigned no particular responsibility or authority and offends his colleagues when he attempts to exercise that nonexistent authority.

I propose that the modern presidential spouse play out her role as the president's conscience. In this role, the president's spouse relates to the president exclusively, serving as his private conscience and acting with complete independence from the body politic (or in our case, the college). The college, the president, and the spouse are all better served by the spouse's acting as her husband's conscience and not as his left hand. The skeptic will ask, "How realistic is it to expect a president's spouse to balance the demands of a career with the undoubted and very real expectations of various college constituencies?" The short answer is that it should not be the responsibility of the *spouse* to achieve

---

[11] Marguerite Walker Corbally, *The Partners: Sharing the Life of a College President* (Danville, Ill.: Interstate Printers & Publishers, 1977), p. 7.

a balance, but rather the responsibility of the *board* to see that she is freed from the "undoubted and very real expectations of (*all*) college constituencies."

In discussing these issues, I must clamber over some very uneven emotional terrain. Situations such as the Denton suicide are tragic. Other situations I describe range in tone from sad to ironic to funny to triumphal to just plain stupid. Because of this, the events and stories which I use to illustrate my thesis cover this same emotional range.

Some of what follows will not strike a responsive chord with some college presidents' spouses, many board of trustees members, and some college presidents. However, I am raising an alarm primarily for the benefit of the college or university (as an institution). Heeding the alarm may well create a collateral benefit for trustees, presidents, and president's spouses; but I warn the palace guard primarily to save the city—not just the palace guard.

CHAPTER 1

I GET NO RESPECT

My wife and I were married in 1970. Nineteen years and two graduate degrees later, Dr. Peggy Williams became President of Lyndon State College (Vermont). Eight years later she became President of Ithaca College (New York). Now forty-plus years after that 1970 marriage, I have concluded my twentieth (and final) year as the president's spouse.

Until 2003 most of my knowledge about being a presidential spouse came from my own experiences, AASCU (American Association of State Colleges and Universities) and CIC (Council of Independent Colleges) conferences, and personal relationships with other presidential spouses. During 2003, I read *The President's Spouse: Volunteer or Volunteered,* a collection of essays by presidential spouses highlighting the results of a NASULGC (National Association of State Universities and Land-Grant Colleges) survey of 138 college and university spouses of presidents/chancellors.[12] This reading led me on to other articles, biographies, and autobiographies and to a

---

[12] J. E. Clodius and D. S. Magrath, eds., *The President's Spouse: Volunteer or Volunteered* (Washington, D.C.: National Association of State Universities and Land-Grant Colleges, 1984).

further and closer look at the literature relating to the role/job of the college president's spouse.

Most of that reading confirmed the impressions I received at my first AASCU meeting in 1989. There are a number of associations which serve and educate presidents (and sometimes their spouses). They also advocate on behalf of their member institutions of higher education. AASCU, CIC, NASULGC, ACE, and AAHE are among the names on a long list of such organizations. The trade organization for boards of trustees is AGB (Association of Governing Boards).

In connection with the annual meeting of AASCU, organizers provide a separate program for spouses. For many years, these programs were largely intended to entertain. The most common activities were house and garden tours, shopping outings, and occasional golf tournaments. When I first attended these events, an attempt was being made to introduce some measure of substance to spouses' programs. At my first AASCU meeting, spouse sessions on "Entertaining at the President's House" and "Packing Tips—Have Plenty of Room Left in Your Baggage to Bring Home Souvenirs of Your Trip" were on the program—among others. Subsequent conferences which I have attended have provided increasingly thought-provoking fare.

At these meetings, there has been a pervasive sense among presidential spouses (clearly and often expressed at spouse sessions) that they are providing substantial and important services to the colleges which their spouses head, and that these colleges do not appreciate and/or properly recognize that service. Rarely will a president's spouse speak publicly about this concern, but when they gather at AASCU and CIC, they speak very freely and frankly among themselves. The emotions expressed range from a vague, undifferentiated unease to feelings of helplessness to indignation and honest anger. Real tears are not the rule, but they do occur. These expressions of emotion stand in stark contrast to most of the essays which appear in *The President's Spouse: Volunteer or Volunteered* and like-minded publications. In the public arena, it has always been OK for a spouse to feel overwhelmed by the work or lonely because her husband president is constantly absent, but it is only in the privacy of the spouses' sessions that spouses express the outrage and/or profound sadness which they believe is caused by the college's insensitivity, hostility, and/or ingratitude. Literature which provides a window on the life of the college president's spouse includes survey-based works (Patricia Justice's *The Role of the University Presidential Spouse,* Marguerite Corbally's *The Partners,* Roberta Ostar's *Public Roles, Private Lives,* and Judith Bressette's *Comparison of the Role of Male and Female Spouses of Presidents*) and autobiographies (Kathleen Koehler's *The Evolving Role of the President's Wife at the University of Michigan,* Muriel Beadle's *Where Has All the Ivy Gone?,* Jean Kemeny's *It's Different at Dartmouth,* and Constance Gee's *Higher Education: Marijuana at the Mansion*). Although the survey-based pieces are more scholarly, the autobiographical materials provide much livelier and revealing reading. Across these materials, the old themes resonate: overwork, underappreciation, and helplessness in the face of unreasonable institutional demands.

Most autobiographical works have been published in post-presidential times—and for obvious reasons. Jean

Kemeny broke with this practice when she wrote *It's Different at Dartmouth.*[13] Her book was unique because her husband, John, was still serving as the president of Dartmouth when the book was published. Her anger, elation, and confusion are everywhere evident; and what she *did* at Dartmouth led pretty directly to how she *felt* about Dartmouth.[14]

Like many current presidential spouses whom I have heard at AASCU and CIC, Kemeny firmly believed that *both* she and her husband had been hired by Dartmouth and that she had a job at the college. The responsibilities of that job (as she envisioned it) included running the president's house, entertaining guests, enhancing alumni relations, and representing both the college and her husband in numerous venues. Within a year after John Kemeny's appointment, Jean Kemeny rocked the academic community by attending (uninvited) a meeting of the faculty. In her view, there was nothing inappropriate about this appearance because she was, by her own description, a spokesperson for the college who needed to have a broad-based knowledge of the state of the Dartmouth College enterprise.

She believed that her presence at events like the faculty meeting would directly save her husband's time and further save the time it would take for him to report the meeting's events to *her*. This attitude assumed that President Kemeny's presence at the faculty meeting

[13] J. Kemeny, *It's Different at Dartmouth* (Brattleboro, Vt.: Stephen Greene Press, 1979).

[14] What she did at and felt about Dartmouth were largely functions of that institution's culture and the attitudes of its Board of Trustees.

would be appropriate and/or welcome and that it would be necessary or desirable for him to report the events of the meeting to Mrs. Kemeny. She concluded that her powers and responsibilities were substantially coextensive with those of her husband in all areas including public relations and, to a lesser extent, academic governance. She also believed that she had a need for and should have access to all information relating to Dartmouth which her husband had. In all of these regards, she acted on her beliefs.

Understandably, the faculty was not wildly enthusiastic about her uninvited participation in their meeting or her perception of her role as it related to them. In doing what she did, Jean ran against the tide of the academic traditions of Dartmouth and just about every other institution of higher education at that time. Because the student body, faculty, and administration were overwhelmingly male, her beliefs and actions inevitably ran afoul of Dartmouth's male traditions as well.

Although she believed herself to be substantially in charge of alumni relations, she had a hard time of it. She described incidents where she had to relate to both overtly sexist and obviously intoxicated alumni. Her responses to alumni bad behavior, whether real or wishful, demonstrated an angry and aggressive streak which is very much at odds with the typical alumni relations persona. By her own description, she relieved her tension by yelling loudly, throwing things around the president's house, and having bi- or tri-annual public outbursts which she described as volcanic.

Her behaviors and Dartmouth's reactions to them caused her to experience emotional highs and lows. She could be positively giddy when describing an interview in which the reporter treated her as the president's equal. Yet, when another reporter wrote about a presidential reception for the dance troupe Pilobolus and failed to give Mrs. Kemeny reportage about her planning and supervision of the event, she became very upset, referring to the female reporter as a "MCP."[15]

She enjoyed being referred to by titles such as "The First Lady of Dartmouth" and "Dartmouth's First Lady and Principal Assistant to the President"[16] and described herself as talented and sophisticated. However, within two pages of declaring herself to be something very special at Dartmouth, she described herself as manic, depressed, unsophisticated, and emotionally unpleasant.[17] At various points in her narrative she laments having given all for her husband while later denying that she had done so.

A special tension electrifies Jean's relationship with the Dartmouth community. Although she makes only infrequent reference to her own education, a substantial portion of her insecurity and anger might have had its wellspring in her lack of traditional indicia of higher education. She attended Smith College for one year before participating in a conference at Princeton. There she met John Kemeny (then a Princeton faculty member), marrying him about a year later. She never returned to Smith. Dartmouth, with all of its real and

[15] Kemeny, *It's Different at Dartmouth*, p. 58.

[16] Ibid., pp. 37, 144–145.

[17] Ibid., p. 176.

imagined intellectual self-satisfaction, must have been a tough place for the girl who quit college. That alone would be enough to make a presidential spouse conflicted in her view of herself.[18]

What was "different" at Dartmouth was the kind of guerrilla-warfare approach which she took to presidential spousehood. It was an "I will do what my gut tells me and let the Devil take the hindmost" attitude. Certainly, some of what she writes is hyperbole, but her overall attitude is that of a partisan— and a partisan without the kind of community sympathy which any successful political guerrilla needs to advance her cause.

She did not appear to have effectively questioned whether her relationships with the college and with her husband were somehow different. She indulged an assumption that her loyalty to her husband translated into an obligation which she had to the college and which the college had, correspondingly, to her. This assumption allowed her to fall into the trap of allowing the traditions of the college (as manifested by the Board of Trustees' attitudes) and her own assumptions about what being the president's wife was, to create the hurly-burly which her life (as she described it) became.

Ultimately, she and many of her sisters in college presidential spousehood came to believe that although they practiced loyalty to husband and college, that college did not honor its corresponding obligation to them. Mrs. Kemeny was not unique in this

---

[18] Had she received her degree from Smith, she might be equally miserable—realizing that she could have done so much more than fending off drunken alumni and hosting receptions.

perspective—or in her overall experience as a presidential spouse. The literature in this area is full of similar complaints. However, because she was so dedicated, smart, and energetic, it was disappointing that she did not make the final step—the step which would cause her to dissociate herself from having obligations to the college (as opposed to having an understanding with her husband). Had she made that step, she could have participated in the affairs of Dartmouth only to the extent she found comfortable, could have supported her husband in whatever manner she (and he) chose, and, most importantly, could have had a life of her own. In doing so she would have transformed herself from being a self-declared agent of the college (a Minister without Portfolio) into a conscience for her husband.

No doubt, Mrs. Kemeny, solely by force of her intellect and personality, could not have adopted a non-college life of her own at the time and under the circumstances she experienced at Dartmouth. Likewise, the Dartmouth Board of Trustees was not likely to encourage her to do so. However, times and circumstances have changed and modern boards of trustees can and must do better than the Dartmouth board did in articulating the role of the president's spouse.

The most curious and useful statement Jean Kemeny makes in her memoir is one which I have not yet seen expressly admitted by any other presidential spouse—in print or in person. She claimed to have entertained feelings of royalty, describing these feelings in terms similar to those used when a person on a diet succumbs to a large piece of triple chocolate cake. She described those feelings as "*queenly*." If her participation in the affairs of Dartmouth was driven by an impulse for that *queenly* feeling, then Dartmouth fully performed its part of the supposed bargain with the occasional fawning and flattery which is described throughout her book. Whatever Dartmouth's opinion of her might have been (assuming one could assay what a college's "opinion" was), her perception was that she was often disliked and/or not respected. Many of her complaints presage the complaints of her twenty-first-century fellow presidential spouses.

There is (and has been) a substantial amount of *queenliness* acted out by presidential spouses of both genders at other colleges and universities over the decades. While Jean Kemeny's enjoyment of her *queenliness* occurred in the 1970s, participants in a 2008 conference of presidential spouses were referred to by one speaker as "community royalty."

The concept of presidential spouses as some form of royalty has a long pedigree. In the *minority* of instances, these royal behaviors are *offensive* (in the sense of seizing command of a situation/college). More often, these behaviors are *defensive*—arising in response to misunderstanding between the spouse and the college community as to the roles and responsibilities of the respective parties. These misunderstandings cause the spouse to feel she is being confronted by the college community. The spouse's defensiveness is then viewed by the college staff as offensive (in the sense of "giving offense").

Whether offensive or defensive, queenly behaviors are symptoms of an impending or ongoing breakdown in the relationship between the spouse and the college. Although such a breakdown can occur without *queenliness*, the presence of queenly behaviors greatly enhances the likelihood of such a breakdown.[19]

Boards should be especially alert to queenly behaviors, because they damage both the college and the spouse. The phenomenon of misinterpreting the relationships among presidents, spouses, and institutions and the consequences of that misinterpretation are hardly new.

Spouses of college presidents, politicians, clergymen, and top-line executives of every stripe have long suffered from cultures in which spouses are given major institutional responsibilities but afforded little clearly defined authority. As they attempt to fulfill these responsibilities, the people whose help they need to get the job done too often sense the spouse's lack of authority and respond accordingly. It is at this point that the spouse realizes that she truly does not get the respect she believes she deserves.

---

[19] Queenly behaviors are not limited to women spouses. Increasingly, male presidential spouses are demonstrating similar behaviors

CHAPTER 2

"EVERYTHING OLD IS NEW AGAIN. . ."[20]

The range of the president's spouse's disenchantment extends across broad spectra of time and causation. Three examples of disenchantments of the wives of powerful men follow. The first is a modern disenchantment caused by a spouse with an offensive queenly style. The second is a nineteenth-century disenchantment caused by cultural norms which bulldozed a very intelligent and well-meaning woman. The third is best described as a disenchantment set in the 1950s but which has been so common from generation to generation and century to century that it is almost allegorical. The breadth of these spectra is littered with broken or bitterly disappointed spouses who deserved better.

---

[20] Peter Allen and Carole Bayer Sager, *Everything Old Is New Again*

A.

YELLOW PLASTIC AND THE LAW OF UNINTENDED CONSEQUENCES

I have already made some observations about spouses' sessions at meetings of AASCU, CIC, and like organizations—including the topics of the first seminars I attended. I would like to take some time to describe one of these seminars. Many years ago while reading a college presidents' conference program, I noted a number of spouse events including garden and house tours. All spouse events were, helpfully, highlighted in pink. I passed on the house and garden tours but was a little teased by a seminar on "Entertaining at the President's House." Although I did not plan any poker games or Super Bowl parties at the President's house, the topic was arguably more interesting than the one on packing suitcases. My agenda was set.

I appeared at the designated time and place and entered a room full of female presidential spouses. There was not another male present (save, possibly, the guy who was cleaning up the coffee cups). At the front of the room stood a very nicely attired woman with an air of substantial self-confidence. She began a well-prepared presentation in which she detailed how she (as the wife of the president of a university) entertained university guests. Her methods involved the keeping of computer records which would have made the Office of Homeland Security envious (had it existed at that time). Guests were cross-referenced to other guests, to their food preferences, to their allergies, to the location of various pieces of entertainment paraphernalia, and to numerous

30

other descriptors (including who drank what and who had "overdone it" at previous events).

Additionally, there were voluminous checklists for physical plant, food service, and administrative staff to complete on a preliminary, interim, and final basis—all of which lists were ultimately to be approved by the speaker. I was amazed by the intrusiveness of some of the guest-data collected and by the complete lack of faith the speaker demonstrated in the university employees from physical plant, food service, and administration, whose responsibility it was to do the work for which they had been hired. I wondered how representatives of those departments would react to this presentation. My guess would be "negative" or, in the alternative, "where can I get one of those union drive cards?" Surely, relations between university staff and this presidential spouse must have been pretty tense.

Toward the end of the scheduled time, the presenter asked for questions from the floor. A woman close by me asked, "What was your worst moment in entertaining for the university?" The presenter's answer came so quickly that it appeared to me that she had answered this question (or told this story) many times before.

She explained that before she had developed the systems which she had just described, there had been a very significant event on what she described as "my campus." Early in this presidential spouse's "tenure," a "very important and generous" (I doubt there is a meaningful distinction between "important" and "generous" in this context) donor was to be entertained by Dr. and Mrs. President on the mezzanine of the library building. Food service, physical plant, and administration staff had made the arrangements.

Mrs. President was on the arm of the "important and generous" donor as they ascended the escalator to the mezzanine of the library building when . . . "Gasp!!!" she exclaimed in a manner which made everyone in the room jump. It sounded as if she had either been pierced between the shoulder blades by a spear or had suffered some terminal intracranial event. "And there they were," she continued in a horrified tone; "at all the place settings were those awful yellow plastic glasses! The ones the *students* drink out of!"

I found her story very funny and would have broken into laughter but for a quick glance around the room. My laughter was instantly stifled. Many in the audience were nodding in silent assent and genuine sympathy. For these folks, the presence of yellow plastic glasses was a very life-altering event. In the life of the presenter, the presence of the yellow plastic glasses mandated a major change in the way in which events at "her university" were planned and executed.

There was no suggestion that the speaker might have conversed with food service personnel about future place settings. The changes were made, the systems and computer programs were effected, and that was that. The likelihood that the changes which she made would prove insulting to the staff and would tend to make Mrs. President's life in the academy unpleasant was of no apparent significance to her. If she had any awareness of negative potential of her failure to collaborate with the college staff, it was completely masked by her manifest condescension to (if not contempt for) the college employees who were responsible for putting on such events.

This is an example of what I call *offensive queenliness*. There was no suggestion in this woman's presentation that she would not have implemented these programs even absent the yellow plastic glasses. For her, this area of university life was her turf simply by reason of her being the president's wife. The glasses were her justification for action, just as the non-incidents in the Gulf of Tonkin were Lyndon Johnson's justification for the commencement of the Viet Nam War and the sinking of the *Maine* became the justification for the Spanish-American War. No matter the reality or the probable consequences—the changes were going to be made—no matter . . .

B.

HELEN MAGILL WHITE

Born in 1853, Helen Magill was one very intelligent and accomplished woman. Her father, the president of Swarthmore, saw to the thorough and rigorous education of all six of his children—including the girls. Helen boasted a number of firsts. She was the only female student to attend Boston Public Latin School in the nineteenth century. She was the first woman to earn a doctorate in the United States: a Ph.D. in Greek and Classical Studies awarded to her in 1877.

Helen passed qualifying examinations at Newham College of Cambridge University (England) in an attempt to accomplish her objective of teaching at the university level. At the time teaching positions at United States universities were not open to women. Although she later passed honors examinations at Newham, her scores were not sufficient to qualify her to teach there. She returned to America where she worked as a secondary school educator in Pennsylvania, Massachusetts, and New Jersey.

In 1887, Helen met Andrew Dickson White at a meeting of the American Social Science Association. He was the first (and former) president of Cornell University. They struck up a friendship and were married in September 1890. At that time, he was in his 60s. She was 37.

From the start of the marriage, Helen knew what she was getting into. The times and the mores were

Victorian. Legally and practically, a woman gave up her identity when she married. By statute, married women could own no property in their own names. Women had not yet won the right to vote. They were expected to bear and raise children and run their households on whatever their husbands saw fit to provide. Women were socially isolated and entirely dependent on their husbands. They were expected to do as they were told. The experiences of husband, family, and love were supposed to be the compensating factors for the isolation and dependency.

Helen was fortunate because Andrew was financially secure and, for the times, progressive in his view of women's opportunities. At Cornell, his stated view of women in higher education could be considered radical: "I had come to believe that where no special difficulties existed, women might well be admitted to university privileges."[21] The women's privileges were not coextensive with those of men. Women were initially housed at Sage College, a separate facility located about a mile from the main campus. When women students complained to White that their segregation was unfair and inconsistent, White countered that, with regard to men and women, "The cases were not the same; that when young women insisted on their right to come and go at all times of the day and night, as they saw fit, without permission, it was like their right to walk from the campus to a beautiful point opposite us on the lake; the right they undoubtedly had, but insurmountable obstacles were in the way; and I showed them that a firm

---

[21] Andrew Dickson White, *The Autobiography of Andrew Dickson White* (New York: The Century Company, 1905), p. 182

public opinion was an invincible barrier to the liberties they claimed."[22] Both the students and Helen had rights but no venue in which to exercise them because of those "insurmountable obstacles" and "invincible barriers."

Helen was the product of the mores of her time. She believed in the intellectual equality of men and women, but she also believed that once a woman was married, her primary duty was to her husband's happiness and contentment. Notwithstanding her academic achievements and independent spirit, Helen tried to settle into a traditional Victorian marriage. She bore Andrew one daughter, Karin. Later, a son was stillborn. Although Andrew managed to write a very long autobiography,[23] none of the events relating to Helen or his children found mention in it because he did not consider them material to the telling of *his* life's story. He placed demands on Helen and expected that she would perform accordingly. At the end of the day, however, she was not considered by Andrew to be sufficiently important to warrant mention in his grand and self-congratulatory work. Although present-day presidents are generally more considerate than Andrew White was, present-day college communities can be just as dismissive of the president's spouse as White was of Helen. As Andrew pursued his public careers in government and the Foreign Service, both he and Helen understood her responsibilities for facilitating his public life. Her biographer, Glenn Altschuler, observed, "Being Mrs. White was a full-time job, and a career was not

---

[22] Ibid., p. 187.

[23] See note 21 above.

compatible, she believed, with raising a family."[24] White depended on Helen to serve as his social secretary, answering correspondence, entertaining guests, and purchasing gifts, and "he did not hesitate to pepper her with instructions."[25] All of this should sound very familiar to many modern college presidents' spouses. From 1897 to 1902 Andrew served as the United States Ambassador to Germany and Helen lived in Berlin, with him. Her role as the ambassador's wife was indistinguishable from that of the presidential spouse. In either of these roles the demands were incessant and gratitude for fulfilling those roles was expressed but rarely—if at all. Altschuler noted that "(e)ven a 'dreadful cough' did not exempt her from her duties as a hostess: she planned a half dozen dinner parties from her bed."[26] Andrew's directions and admonitions to Helen even extended beyond the grave. When Helen spoke to him of her wish to remain in Ithaca (the locus of Cornell) should he predecease her, "he (White) lectured her about Mrs. Nott of Union College" (widow of Union President Eliphalet Nott), whose house became a center of disaffection against her husband's successor—"her likes and dislikes . . . held with a conscientiousness from the catastrophe of one gifted woman's criticisms."[27]

---

[24] G. C. Altschuler, *Better Than Second Best: Love and Work in the Life of Helen Magill* (Champaign, Ill.: University of Illinois Press, 1990), p. 113.

[25] Ibid., pp. 113–114

[26] Ibid.

[27] Ibid., p. 123. In comfortable disregard of White's wishes, Helen remained in Ithaca after his death. Among other activities, she attended doctoral-level Greek classes at Cornell. She frequently challenged and criticized her professor and became so irritating that she was eventually asked to leave the class. From the points of view of many Cornell

All of this took a toll on Helen, just as it takes a toll on many presidential spouses in twenty-first-century America. These stresses affected her physical and mental health. They profoundly complicated her relationships with her husband, her daughter, and her extended family. It was hard to be intelligent, talented, and quick and, at the same time, be monumentally bored. Helen became, by any definition, a world-class nag. She superintended every aspect of her daughter Karin's life as a girl, as an adolescent, and even as an adult. Karin understandably resented this interference and was, for the majority of her life, substantially estranged from her mother. Only in Helen's final years did she and Karin negotiate a working truce.

Helen's relationship with Andrew became worse than her relationship with Karin. Eventually, the only common ground between them was argument. They argued vehemently about everything and nothing. They were in the midst of a very nasty disagreement when Andrew died. For some time Karin held her mother responsible for her father's death. By the end of her life, Helen had been pretty well beaten down.

As she aged, the consequences of *"defensive queenliness"* became more manifest. Crammed into a corner by the mores of her time and unable to find an effective outlet for her significant abilities, she exhausted those abilities by destroying her relationships with the people and entities which should have buoyed

professors and administrators, Helen had become a significant embarrassment. Later, her decision to move to Maine to be with her sister was undoubtedly well received at Cornell.

her up—her husband, her daughter, and Cornell University. Hers was not a life to be emulated.

Helen died in Maine at the age of 90. For several years before her death she was cared for, in Maine, by her daughter Karin. Helen's last request, that she be buried next to Andrew at Sage Chapel on the Cornell campus, was granted—partially. She was buried near him, but not next to him.

Still, the misery Helen endured suggests a road map for others. Using that map, the modern presidential spouse may be able to avoid the many tortured detours and dead ends which bedeviled Helen's life. In much of this misery Helen did not have much of a choice. The social mores of her time dissuaded her from pursuing her own career.

Notwithstanding the fact that she could have continued her intellectual life in public education, she "gave it all up" to help Andrew as a traditional Victorian wife was expected to do. The phrase "gave it all up for the college" continues to resonate at spouse sessions of AASCU, ACE, and CIC, even today.

Arguably, had she not married, she could have pursued a career in education (probably at the public secondary level and possibly at a women's college). However, Helen wanted to live the full life of a Victorian wife, and in seeking it, she cut herself off from those activities of the mind which gave her vitality. What she "gave up" was her happiness and her life.

The modern college presidential spouse has (or can forge) an option to pursue and exploit her own talents. By doing so she provides first for herself, creating a stronger and more vibrant person who can then better support the president. Helen gave up the exploitation of her talents to serve Andrew and suffered horribly for it. With the help of enlightened boards of trustees, the modern spouse of a college president can, by limiting her loyalties and labors to her spouse and herself, better serve both the president and the college.

Again the skeptic interjects, "But for the modern college president's spouse, this is simply not realistic." A relevant definition of "realistic" references appreciation of things as they actually are. To that skeptic, I rejoin in the words of Robert Kennedy, "Some men see things as they are and say why. I dream things that never were and say why not?" The concept of an independent president's spouse, beholden to no relationship save her relationship with the president, is realistic to a few, but a dream to far too many. It is time to change the dreamers to realists; and boards of trustees must be the change agents.

C.

THE MINISTER'S WIFE

Today, there are many more male college presidents' spouses than there were in the 1980s. They too speak at national meetings. Occasionally their laments echo those of the women I have described, but largely they do not. There is a fair amount of literature on the subject of the lot of the college president's spouse, and most of it was written by or about women because virtually all presidential spouses were women at the time this literature was published. Frequently this literature compares the role of the presidential spouse to that of the minister's wife (in the sense of the church minister's wife). Many presidential spouses of my acquaintance bridle at this comparison. If the wife of my minister in the 1950s was what these spouses were thinking of, I can understand their feelings.

In my youth, my minister's wife was rather short, very quiet, and decidedly gray. She dressed very modestly in colors which were all drawn from camouflage. Unless you looked very carefully, you could not see her at all. She sat in the back of the church and listened to the Reverend's sermons with an attitude which I could never quite figure out. She was either concentrating with great intensity on her husband's words—or she was sleeping. I often saw her doing things, but rarely saying anything. Whatever could not be done because of a shortage in the collection plate fell to Mrs. Reverend to do—and by God, she tried to get it done. Although she smiled beatifically whenever she was at the side of her husband, she never had an opinion

41

about anything. Overall, she projected an aura of profound sadness. I recall one Sunday when we were called upon to offer prayers for the sick. One of the sick was Mrs. Reverend, but until her name was mentioned in the service, no one had noticed that she was not there. It was really quite embarrassing.

It is this passive, mute, self-sacrificing caricature sometimes adopted by boards and college communities as their model of the ideal college president's wife that drives these spouses wild. This is not a happy model for the presidential spouse of the twenty-first century

Although the modern presidential spouse frequently says more than the Mrs. Reverend of my youth, the value which the college community places on her contributions is often equivalent to the value the congregation placed on Mrs. Reverend's contributions— that is to say, "not much." At the same time these very same communities, boards, and sometimes presidents expect (and in many cases demand) extensive spouse services.[28] In such circumstances it is easy for a spouse to become conflicted, confused, and bitter. Neither the passive, mute, self-sacrificing model, nor the victim-of-traditions model, nor the whip-that-staff-into-order model well serves the modern presidential spouse.

I attended many more of AASCU/CIC meetings over the years. I heard a lot of speakers and audience members, many of whom were highly competent and credentialed women. Many of these women had given up their careers in order to help their husbands succeed as college presidents. Admittedly, this was not a valid sample for statistical purposes, but most of the spouses

---

[28] In some situations the expectations are self-imposed by the spouse.

who were talking were saying the same thing: "I gave up my career to help my husband. I gave everything I had to the college, and they hate me (or have no respect for me, etc.)."

In an alternative formulation, some said, "I don't know what the college would have done without me. None of them know how to entertain in the manner in which it should be done. I'm the best ambassador to the outside community and the best fund-raiser they have. I would think that they would appreciate me, but they don't."

How did the presidential spouse get into the unholy spot? How might she or he get out of it—and to where?

David A. Williams

CHAPTER 3

"WHY DO THEY HATE ME?"
—TURF WARS

It is hard to imagine any activity that a presidential spouse could undertake on behalf of the college which is not replete with potential for offending some member or members of the college community. Initially I thought of addressing only the sensibilities of college employees but later realized that the potential for offense extends well beyond the community of employees of the college.

An analogy may be drawn between a college community and a challenged urban neighborhood. In each instance there is a finite amount of turf and that turf is allocated among competing groups and individuals. In the urban setting, gangs may define their respective turfs physically. Boundaries are subject to skirmishes. Territories are defined, contended, and redefined.

On the college campus, the various turfs are not often defined or revised by physical conflict, but more subtle forms of marking and defending do occur. The faculty is very aware of its dominion over matters academic. This academic turf covers issues of curriculum, promotion and tenure, demotion and termination, allocation of resources which customarily are used to support academics, determinations of who will qualify for the receipt of various degrees,

45

assignment of faculty to course offerings, and myriad other related issues.

Administration has its turf. The Vice President for Finance usually does not want someone from Student Services telling her how available resources should be allocated. Supplications are fine; suggestions are okay; demands are unwelcome. This is so because there never is enough money, and the folks in Finance know better than others how these scarce resources should be divided. The provost, of course, knows that administration exists solely as a support structure for the faculty—and is, in fact, subordinate to the needs and desires of the faculty.[29] In this view of the campus world, the person in Finance is a bean counter who has no sense of the true nature and mission of the college.

Legal counsel is something of a shaman. He knows all of the awful things which can befall the institution if the right offerings and rituals are not made and performed. Because counsel cannot generally explain the real necessity of the offerings and rituals in language anyone else can understand (or because no one is willing to learn legal vocabulary), he has special powers to make other members of the college community do things which they do not want to do—all in the name of "the law." Legal counsel thus has a large turf which is hard to limit.

Staff, too, have turf; and they defend it vigorously. The clerical staff know that the institution could not possibly operate without their individual and collective

---

[29] See below, p. 175, quotation beginning "Universities began, in the middle ages, as a conglomeration of Masters around whom groups of students clustered. . . ."

common sense. In their view, faculty members are simply people with far too much time to think about far too little. As a result, faculty are seen as living in a sort of never-never land which can be maintained only by the diligence and practicality which clerical staff bring to the campus. Buildings and Grounds people have special, practical skills without which the institution would collapse. A dean is not seen as having either the stomach or the skill to unblock a toilet. A faculty member is certainly incompetent to change a light bulb (without the assistance of a several-person subcommittee). Students believe that by matriculating they have become voting members of an educational cooperative. Their participation in the operation of the cooperative is, of course, voluntary and generally part-time. However, any decision which is perceived as adverse to students' interests prompts calls for "a vote" on its efficacy and implementation. Thus, students assert general authority over any part of the turf which affects them—socially, intellectually, or financially.

Although there is some hyperbole in the foregoing, strains of our shared experience on American college campuses must be recognized. Almost every single bit of authority or turf is claimed at various times by two or three groups. A decision to raise tuition will be seen by the board as a necessary evil, by faculty as a source of needed money to enhance the learning environment, by staff as a pool from which to fund long-overdue salary/benefit enhancements, and by students as acts 1, 2, and 3 of "The Highwayman."

Into this contentious environment steps the president's spouse. She is newly minted, eager, sincere, talented, and—no matter how experienced she may have been at some other institution—massively uninformed as to the internal politics of the institution which her husband has been selected to head. This spouse is welcomed with warmth apparently equal to that afforded the new president, but without the respect which grows out of a recognition of the president's actual power.

Immediately upon commencement of the new presidency, various people will suggest activities in which the new president's spouse could engage which would be helpful to the college. These suggestions are generally made by people whose turf would not be affected by the spouse's acting on the suggestion. For example, the spouse of a board member might suggest that the presidential spouse undertake a campus beautification initiative. A business manager might suggest that the presidential spouse teach a course. A board member might suggest the president's spouse help out with development work.

In each instance the presidential spouse is being invited to step onto someone else's turf. The Campus Beautification initiative implies that the campus is not adequately beautiful. If that is so, someone in Buildings and Grounds has not been paying enough attention to issues of campus beauty. Since the academy is so thoroughly "turfed-out," someone is bound to be offended or threatened by the beautification initiative.

If the spouse accepts the challenge of teaching a course at the college, some existing faculty member is not going to teach that course. Even if the course is not one which has previously been offered at that campus, the offering necessarily limits some other offering which existing faculty members have wanted to teach. Now the president's spouse is on faculty turf—and faculty are not always welcoming and can be judgmental.

R. Weintraub in an essay titled "Selecting a President – Paths and Potholes" observed that "Search Committees have learned the hard way that a departmental appointment committee will dig in its heels if even a suggestion is made that the president's spouse, male or female, is a suitable candidate for the department."[30]

There are exceptions to this rule, but they are very rare. Robert O. Keohane, husband of Nannerl Keohane, joined the faculty at Duke following the appointment of his wife as president of that university. Robert Keohane, however, was famous in his own right as a political science scholar, having taught at Swarthmore, Stanford, Brandeis, and Harvard before joining the Duke faculty. There was little doubt that Robert would have been welcomed by Duke whether his wife was its president or not. The same can be said for David Skorton's (President of Cornell University) wife, Robin Davisson. A small portion of her curriculum vitae is set out below.[31]

---

[30] R. Weintraub, "Selecting a President—Paths and Potholes," in *Beyond the Falling Sky: Surmounting Pressures on Higher Education*, ed. T. M. Stauffer (Washington, D.C.: American Council on Education, 1981), p. 107.

[31] "Professor Davisson's research focuses on the basic mechanisms of function, control and signaling in the cardiovascular system in health and disease. Her investigations employ the interdisciplinary approach of 'functional genomics,' a new endeavor at the interface of classical physiology and molecular genetics. She has published numerous original research and review articles and book chapters, and has given invited presentations throughout the United States as well as in South America, Europe and Asia.

Hiring the president's world-class academic spouse may create unintended difficulties for that spouse. World-class academics became world-class because of their surpassing interest in a particular discipline. If President X's wife is a Nobel laureate in economics and is hired as a professor of economics, she will certainly have a greater interest in and dedication to matters of economics than she will in matters of social entertainment and development. If the college is accustomed to a president's wife who bakes cookies, entertains faculty wives, and accompanies the president on long development road shows, it will probably become disappointed in its world-class economist. She

---

"Her research has been funded by competitive grants from the U.S. National Institutes of Health, the American Heart Association and private industry. In addition, her research has earned multiple awards, including the Harry Goldblatt Award in Cardiovascular Research from the American Heart Association and the Henry Pickering Bowditch Award from the American Physiological Society. She has also won awards from the American Society of Hypertension, the International Society of Hypertension, and the International Congress of Physiological Sciences.

"Professor Davisson has been actively involved in service to national and international organizations and journals. She is currently chair of programming and serves on the steering committee for the American Physiological Society (Neural Control and Autonomic Regulation Section) and serves on the leadership and the programming committees of the American Heart Association High Blood Pressure Research Council. She also serves on the editorial boards of Hypertension, Physiological Genomics, and the American Journal of Physiology: Regulatory, Integrative and Comparative. From 2003-2005, she was associate editor for Experimental Physiology." Retrieved from Cornell University website: http://www.vet.cornell.edu/labs/davisson/LabMembers/RobinDavisson.cfm (accessed January 1, 2008). Davisson's CV has been updated since I originally accessed it. It is offered in its original form only to provide an example of a prominent tenured faculty member's typical CV.

now has double trouble. Her relationship with the campus suffers from her dedication to the study of economics and her scholarship suffers from the attention which she feels she must give the campus in areas unrelated to her academic expertise.[32]

If delivering a paper at a major meeting of economists conflicts with "the rivalry" football game of the year (a game attended by many major donors), which master does she serve? Either way she loses. Either way she is unfairly stressed. Either way she incurs the displeasure of some campus constituency.

The Keohane and Davisson situations stand in stark contrast to situations in which the new president's spouse is granted a faculty position with tenure as a part of the quid pro quo for the president's services—rather than as quid pro quo for her anticipated services as a professor. When a quick review of the president's spouse's CV reveals little teaching experience other than that which occurred in institutions where and at the times when the president was serving as president, faculty resentment is nearly inevitable.

An example of this phenomenon has recently occurred at Vanderbilt University. Vanderbilt's now departed president, E. Gordon Gee, had served presidencies at the University of West Virginia (1981 to 1985), the University of Colorado (1985 to 1990), the Ohio State University (1990 to 1997), Brown University

---

[32] Constance Gee, whose adventures as a university president's spouse are discussed in Chapter 3 (below), firmly believes that her responsibilities as a social host and development supporter seriously interfered with her scholarship.

David A. Williams

(1997 to 2000), and Vanderbilt (2000 to 2007). He has now returned to the Ohio State presidency.[33]

In 1993, during Gee's first presidency at Ohio State, his wife-to-be, Constance Bumgarner, completed her Ph.D. in Art Education at Penn State. She then took a teaching position at Ohio State specializing in Art Education Policy issues. There she met and later married the OSU president. When E. Gordon Gee moved to Brown in 1998, Constance moved with him and began teaching a course entitled "Public Policy, the Arts and Arts Education," supervised independent studies, and advised students.[34] It was rumored that Gordon Gee had attempted to negotiate a tenured position for his wife but that the Brown faculty had refused.[35]

Constance objected to my inclusion of any material gleaned from the B.A. Zeff *Village Voice* article (see footnote 34) on the grounds that the author was extremely biased and that even mention of the article would give it undeserved legitimacy. I hold no brief for the article's accuracy or inaccuracy. Even if the article was entirely false, the acknowledged facts that Constance was E. Gordon's wife and a Brown faculty

---

[33] As of this writing Gee has resigned the presidency of OSU, joined the law faculty there and then returned to the presidency of West Virginia University.

[34] Constance Gee, Curriculum Vitae, Vanderbilt University website, September 2007. No longer available online. See Appendix A, below.

[35] B. A. Zeff, "Premature Evacuation," *Village Voice*, February 11, 2000, http://www.villagevoice.com/2000-08-01/art/premature-evacuation/2/ (accessed March 1, 2013); posts by newengland in "Gordon Gee Was Fired," http://groups.google.com/g/6427feea/t/b8d8c9f89bf0e171/d/8fc717b8a3f86455 (accessed March 1, 2013).

member during her husband's presidency contributed significantly to the discomfort Constance Gee experienced.

During his service at Brown, controversy raged over Gordon Gee's extensive and expensive renovations to the president's house, his disbanding of an arts group, and Constance Gee's abilities or inabilities as a college-level teacher.[36] A little more than two years after Gee had taken the Brown presidency, he resigned it to assume the chancellorship of Vanderbilt. As a part of the negotiations for this new position, Constance Gee was appointed Associate Professor of Public Policy and Education—a tenured position. Her curriculum vitae was available on the Vanderbilt website but has since been removed. A copy of that CV can be found as Appendix A below. I will leave it to the reader's judgment to discern if substantial similarities exist between the typical tenured faculty member's CV and that of Dr. Gee.

Although Gordon Gee's development work kept him in good stead at Vanderbilt, criticisms of his management style and of Constance's behaviors (see below) caused him to accept an Ohio State offer and return to Columbus.. The problems of both Gees placed serious strains on their marriage. On February 28, 2007, the *Nashville Po*st reported that the Gees had agreed upon a divorce. Gordon was headed back to Columbus and Constance did not appear to be going with him. Until recently, she continued to be listed as an Associate Professor—with tenure—at Vanderbilt.

---

[36] Zeff, "Premature Evacuation"; newengland, "Gordon Gee Was Fired."

David A. Williams

Given the risk that Constance might remain in her tenured position after E. Gordon's departure and/or the potential cost of buying her out, boards should be extremely circumspect in their negotiations concerning presidential spouses and tenured positions, lest what was originally thought to be a small side agreement in the president's contract becomes a permanent irritant to faculty relations. Application of the same standards for tenure to the new president's spouse as are applied to other tenured hires should be the rule. Negotiation of tenure for a spouse who was not tenured previously should be taboo. Even a previously tenured spouse should be subject to an honest promotion and tenure review by the faculty of the hiring college.

Many faculty members have been standing in the tenure line for a long time. They have had to demonstrate teaching, research, publishing, and service experience to advance in that line. Many colleagues have fallen by the wayside trying to attain tenure. If, suddenly, a person whose résumé would at best have qualified him for a non-tenured teaching position is granted tenure—without peer review and without otherwise demonstrating his qualifications—there will most likely be hell to pay. For all practical purposes the spouse might just as well have cut into the cafeteria line in the faculty dining room—although he would probably be more popular for cutting the cafeteria line than cutting the tenure line.

If the presidential spouse starts hanging around the development office, offering to do work which is not presently being done or raising development issues which are not currently under consideration, the suggestion is that the development staffers are not doing their jobs. Whether the spouse is then seen as a helper or a spy is unsettled and thus unsettling to the staff. Further, the development staffers see themselves as trained, educated, and experienced in the development field. If the president's spouse is not viewed as having similar training, education, and experience, relations can become very difficult—and difficulty quickly morphs into liability in development circles. If her credentials are superior to those of the existing development staff, a different set of unsettling issues arises. Either way, one side will feel threatened or the other mistrusted or resented.

Although female presidential spouses are more likely to be ensnared in turf problems (because numerically there are more female than male presidential spouses and further because fewer male spouses give up their careers to become presidential spouses), males are not immune.

Shortly after my wife became the president of Lyndon State College she told me about a flag problem the college was having. I did not need to be told because the president's house overlooked the campus—including an immense flagpole. One of the campus landmarks was this very tall flagpole. The pole was erected in honor of T. N. Vail, one of the founders of AT&T, on whose estate the college was built. Vail was an occasional visitor to this particular estate. In order to announce his presence up on the hill, Vail would fly a large American flag on a very tall flagpole, thereby inviting the locals to come and visit. After Vail donated the estate to the college for its new campus, a newer, taller flagpole was erected. It stands 132 feet tall and remains the tallest in Vermont.

During my wife's first year at Lyndon, the flag halyard broke. It failed at the point where it connected to the lower corner of the flag. The balance of the halyard fell to the ground, with its weight holding the top corner of the flag to the pulley at the top of the flagpole.

Connected by only one corner and subject to the vigorous winds of the Passumpsic Valley, the flag quickly became torn and disfigured. Various efforts to retrieve the flag while maintaining the halyard were tried; all failed. Arrows with strings attached were shot through the flag; a National Guard helicopter was requested; and a volunteer pole climber appeared. Although each proposed solution had potential, none worked out. Given the tremendous height of the pole, the tattered flag was visible across the community. Eventually, community members with a sense of flag etiquette began to complain. Lyndon State College had a flag problem and no apparent solution.

In the long-past days of my youth, I had been a flyer of kites. In my young adulthood I had been a sailor of boats (and thus a tier of knots), a chain-sawyer of wood, and an occasional climber of rocks. From this seemingly unrelated set of experiences, I was able to assemble a Rube Goldberg device consisting of a nylon, parafoil-type kite, two carabineers, a pulp hook, and various lengths of light nylon line. When an appropriately windy day arrived, the kite lifted the pulp hook to the level of the flag. The pulp hook snagged the corner of the flag. The kite was released from the hook and flew away from the pole. The pulp hook was then pulled to the ground bringing the flag and, more importantly, the halyard with it.[37] The flag was properly retired. A new halyard was spliced into the old one and run through the pulley atop the pole. A new flag was hoisted and Old Glory once again proudly waved over campus and community.

The retrieval of the flag and halyard was met with general praise and thanks which emboldened me to undertake other projects. Although the president's house commanded a spectacular 180-degree view of the mountains to the east, south, and west, there was no place outside the house either to entertain or simply to sit and enjoy the view. Ever mindful of the resource constraints of any college, my wife and I proposed building a deck on the house at no expense to the college. The proposal was accepted; the materials were purchased at our expense. I started the construction.

Very shortly after the commencement of the work, folks from Buildings and Grounds were on site and strongly critical of my construction techniques. Being the son of an engineer and the constructor of a few decks, I was pretty confident of my methodology. Nonetheless, I prudently disassembled the materials and deferred to the expertise of the Building and Grounds crew.

Although I initially thought of the two experiences as springing from the same source, I later realized that they were clearly distinguishable—first by college employees and later by me. The flag problem involved a situation which was unique. There was nothing in the "Maintenance Procedures Handbook" to deal with this one. All reasonable efforts had been diligently made by

---

[37] I was greatly assisted in this project by Lyndon State College's then Chief Financial Officer, Cornell Frank

responsible college employees, but the problem remained. The campus community would have accepted any effective solution whether it came from me or anyone else. The field was open and I took it.

The deck incident was different. There were plenty of guys in Buildings and Grounds who knew how to build decks—good decks and probably better decks than I would have built.[38] There was something in the "Maintenance Procedures Handbook" to deal with this issue. It was not unique. By starting the deck I was tromping squarely on Buildings and Grounds turf. I should not have been there and moved as quickly as possible to get off.

The turf trap is harder still to avoid if the predecessor presidential spouse was actively involved in the life of the institution. Such a spouse will generally be recollected as a saintlike figure whose dedication to and sacrifice for the college will "long be remembered." The new spouse thus labors in the shadow (or perhaps in the vacuum) of the predecessor presidential spouse and often tries to match or exceed her predecessor's accomplishments. Upon closer examination, however, the new spouse may discover that her predecessor's enshrinement in the pantheon of dedication and sacrifice occurred contemporaneously with her departure from the campus—and her withdrawal from contested turf.

In one instance I followed a spouse who was very active in campus affairs. In the other I followed a spouse who initially was very involved, but who later became alienated from the college community and moved to

---

[38] The deck they built was terrific. I attended an event on that deck fifteen-plus years later and it was still terrific.

another state. In both instances I received the impression that each felt ill done by the college she sought to serve. Although I know it was difficult for them, in an unexpected way their experiences and relations with the respective colleges made it easier for me to strike out on my own.

The more the presidential spouse involves herself in work which is the responsibility of someone already working for the college, the greater the potential for resentment. As the spouse tries to be of greater assistance to the institution and that resentment begins to surface, there is a temptation to do more as a means of demonstrating loyalty and dedication. This course of action becomes the equivalent of Br'er Rabbit's fighting with the tar baby.[39] Eventually, the bewildered spouse asks herself the unfortunate question, "Why do they hate me?"

The pain and discomfort experienced by the spouse in this situation stem from the failure of the spouse, the president, and the institution to understand their proper relationships. The spouse views herself as an extension of the president—a Minister without Portfolio to the college's internal and external constituencies. Members of the institution see the spouse as a person utterly without authority or responsibility who is usurping previously allocated turf. In the worst of these situations the president finds himself defending and supporting the spouse who, ideally, should be supporting and encouraging him.

The risks to which the president's spouse is exposed, and those to which the college is exposed because of the acts and omissions of the president's spouse, do not

---

[39] This Cherokee myth also appears in the Tales of Uncle Remus.

cease when one exits the college gate. Although the intracollegiate environment provides a fertile field for spouse-endured and spouse-created discontent, the larger community is no less troublesome. The potential for difficulty can run in counter directions. The president's spouse can be disliked, disrespected, and depressed because of the reputation of the college in the larger community. Likewise, the college can be disliked, disrespected, and depressed because of the reputation of the president's spouse in that same community. Given the various constituencies of that larger community, both difficulties can be occurring in different parts of the community simultaneously.

The president's spouse can generate discontent beyond the campus simply by her treatment of college employees in their college work. All college employees go home after work and live in town. Town/gown problems often arise because of the communication of information from college employees to their neighbors. If Ms. President's Spouse is mean-spirited and condescending to the food service personnel, the friends and neighbors of those personnel will know about it—as will *their* friends and neighbors.

Still worse is the situation in which the president's spouse is not mean-spirited or condescending but is portrayed as such by a discontented employee. That false reputation may put down roots in the town community. The more active the spouse is in college affairs and the more she interacts with, and directs, college employees in their work, the more likely it is that a negative impression (be that a true impression or a false one) will arise in the larger community. Once that has happened, the spouse becomes a distraction to the real business of the college because she will feel a need to defend herself or the president will have to defend her.

The group of nonemployee college individuals with whom the president's spouse most commonly interacts is the alumni. These folks cannot and should not be ignored. The alumni who stay in touch with the college are ones who most frequently provide financial and other forms of support to the college. But whose job is it to pay attention to these loyal alumni? I submit that it is the college's job—not the spouse's job. Charming, witty, attractive, and skilled development employees can do this job better than the spouse. They will not be criticized by faculty and staff for their speech, attire, or forthrightness because this is their job. Their activities are not just the exercises of a Minister without Portfolio.

There is also a slice of the alumni group made up of those who never really commenced from college to life. These folks return to Alma Mater at age 50 anticipating the same kinds of activities in which they indulged at age 20—and we all pretty much know what these activities are. Jean Kemeny describes her interactions with some of this type of alumni in *It's Different at Dartmouth*. It is a lot easier for a spouse to shrug off bad-boys behaviors if she, like them, is simply a guest of the college—not a representative of the college. Likewise she is less likely to offend if her role does not impel or require her to defend the college's policies and practices.

Another area of potential difficulty involves the adoption and practice of religion. In the early twenty-first century, religion has again become a greater force for divisiveness than it is for unity. I believe that a presidential spouse's choice of religion or denomination as well as her choices of how to practice that religion are absolutely her own business and are well beyond the call or criticism of the college community or the larger community.

Nonetheless, if ABC College is affiliated with the XYZ church and if Ms. President's Spouse chooses to join a different church, her choice will more likely go unnoticed if she does not hold a prominent role in college affairs. Even if the spouse does join the "right" denomination, practices within that denomination may differ widely from church to church. Recent divisions within the Episcopal and Baptist churches serve as examples.

What happens when the national church bars homosexuals from the priesthood, but the local church welcomes them? Is the spouse who joins the local church to be seen as bestowing a college imprimatur on the local policy in defiance of the national church? The more closely she is identified with the everyday affairs of the college, the more her actions will be seen as representations of college positions—not representations of her own conscience. This is not right, it is just true.

A college need not be affiliated with a particular religion or denomination to create faith-based problems for the college, its president, or its president's spouse. Most private colleges in America have some Christian tradition. That tradition may have arisen because of the importance and prominence of a central building on campus, the longstanding religious predilections of the student body, a history of some kind of missionary activity, or the very publicly stated religious beliefs of a major donor (among many others). What happens to support for the college when the president's spouse actively practices some non-Christian faith? Again, the probability of discontent rises as the spouse becomes more closely identified with the regular business of the college and diminishes the less visible she is in college affairs.

Other areas of potential trouble involve charitable causes, the selection of local merchants (or the avoidance of them), and the reliance upon local public services. If the president's spouse elects to work for or do development work for Planned Parenthood, does this reflect a college endorsement of abortion? Of family planning? Of the use of birth control devices? In legal terms the answers are, "Of course not"; "Of course not"; and "Of course not." In practical terms, should this spouse's activities be conjoined with an arrangement in which she is paid by the college for college-related activities, criticism by community members opposed to abortion, family planning, and the use of birth control devices is pretty nigh inevitable.

The "Lake Wobegon®" resident who buys his car from a dealership in Minneapolis rather than buying it in Lake Wobegon is a regular target of Garrison Keillor's humor. If the wife of the president of Lake Wobegon College (LWC) works in Minneapolis and buys a car there, she will likely avoid the sharpest barbs of local disapproval. However, if she has an office at LWC and is prominent in the affairs of the college, she will be fair game when she buys that car in Minneapolis (rather than buying from good old Clarence Bunsen®). [40]

---

[40] G. Keillor, *A Prairie Home Companion®*, various references. Used with permission.

So, too, local merchants and service suppliers who, for years, have done business with the college may find that business lost to a competitor. If that decision is the responsibility of a college purchasing agent, the decision will be understood—even if it is not appreciated. If the fingerprints of the president's spouse are on the decision, the resentment will likely be more firmly held and personal.

When the president's spouse calls upon public services, such as the police, she can call as a member of the general public or as the President's Wife. For the very occasional call, it will probably make no difference how the spouse identifies herself. However, should repeat calls be necessary (e.g. noise complaints on late spring evenings), the close identification of the caller with the college and its president will initially elicit "special attention" and later elicit "status-based" resentment. In all of these matters, the higher the level of status to which the spouse pretends and the lower the status of the community member with which the spouse is dealing (or the lower the spouse's perception of the community member's status), the greater the potential for resentment against both the college and the spouse.

Issues of nomenclature and social status stalk the presidential spouse in even the simplest social situations. From the beginning of her existence as a presidential spouse, she will be introduced and will introduce herself to others. She will also interact with community members in situations in which it is generally unnecessary to introduce herself. In each of these situations, the opportunities for giving offense abound.

The situation with the least downside potential is the introduction of the spouse to a third person by someone who knows her. Usually the introducer will identify the spouse as, "Frieda Frothammer, President Frothammer's wife." The introducer has offered Frieda a metaphorical pedestal. She can accept this offer by standing a little taller, puffing slightly, and saying, very slowly, "How do you do?" This course of action may fulfill a positive stereotype in the sensibilities of the new spouse and probably create a negative one in the sensibilities of the person to whom the spouse has been introduced. A social order is being established here in which the spouse has placed herself just a bit higher in the order of persons than the person to whom she has been introduced. Played in its extreme form, the person making the introduction insinuates her superiority to the person to whom the spouse was just introduced simply because she (knowing the spouse) is closer to her. The more *queenly* the self-image of the presidential spouse, the more likely this scenario will play out, leaving the person who was introduced feeling put down. Since this was her first interaction with the presidential spouse, the impression is likely to last.

The spouse can avoid this trap by replying, "Oh, it's so very nice to meet you, Mrs. Dillingham. Please call me Frieda" (and mean it). This response deconstructs the offered social pecking order and will predispose Mrs. Dillingham more kindly to the president's wife down the road. However, the spouse should be careful of using a first name or nickname which is inappropriate to the setting. The disaster which will follow on the spouse responding, "Oh it's so very nice to meet you, Mrs. Dillingham. Please call me Love Muffin," is predictable.

The cuter the nickname, the more suspect its use. Since the spouse is usually starting anew in the college community, she can pretty much adopt whichever name she thinks will work best.

The issues are somewhat different when the president introduces his wife to others. Some of the potential issues arise as a function of what the president calls himself. If he is generally known on the campus as "Frank," there is no downside to his introducing her as "my wife, Frieda Frothammer," leaving it to her to say, "Oh just call me Frieda." My wife preferred to be known generally by her first name, "Peggy." This gave me the opportunity to respond to any introduction by saying, "Oh, just call me Mr. Peggy." That line almost always drew a laugh, lightening up the introduction.

If he is known as "President Frothammer" or "Dr. Frothammer," the issues are different, depending on the attitude of the observer. If the president is known as "Dr. Frothammer" and she as "Frieda," there will be critics who will consider her status diminished by the informality of her name. If she opts for "Ms. Frothammer" (or in the appropriate circumstance "Dr. Frothammer"), she may be seen by other critics as "setting herself above others." Adopting different names for different constituencies can be difficult and dangerous. In my opinion, the more informal the president and his spouse can be in self-identification, the better.

Further examples of nonemployee community members who can be and are offended by active presidential spouses include college board of trustees members (and more particularly board members' spouses), foundations and other non-alumni development targets, and the media. The legal and public-relations consequences of the president's spouse speaking for the college can be immense. In my studies of this issue, I have found few examples of presidents' spouses bringing colleges to grave woe by public statements, but they do occur.[41]

Factors as apparently remote as the president's spouse's occupation can come into play. Aaron Podolefsky, the president of Central Missouri, lost out on a contract renewal despite his positive performance. Among the possible reasons for nonrenewal cited by Alan Scher Zagier of the Associated Press was "Ronnie Podolefsky's (the president's wife and an attorney) representation of six female high school students who sued the local school district and a former coach for alleged sexual misconduct . . . The civil case remains pending though the accused teacher has since resigned in exchange for prosecutors dropping criminal sex abuse charges."[42] This action by the president's spouse apparently "created a fissure in Warrensburg, a conservative bedroom community for nearby Whiteman Air Force Base."[43]

---

[41] At one presidential inauguration at which the new president's spouse was invited to speak, she referred to the college faculty and staff as the college's "worker bees." That line was long remembered—long after the president was hustled out of town.

[42] A. S. Zagier, "University of Central Missouri's President's Ouster Raises Questions," *Columbia Missourian*, October 29, 2009, http://www.Columbiamissourian.com/stories/2009/10/29central-missouri-university-presid (accessed December 1, 2009). Reprinted with permission of the Associated Press, 2012.

[43] Ibid. Reprinted with permission of the Associated Press, 2012.

In all of these examples, a complicated linkage between the president's spouse and the larger community operates. The linkage is complicated because the relationship of the spouse to the community (like her relationship to the college) is multifaceted. The provost's wife or the biology professor's wife can normally incur the larger community's wrath or disrespect only in relation to *her own* actions. The community's relationship with her will have very little, if anything, to do with her relationship to the college. The college will not be harmed by her actions because she is not seen as a representative of the college (absent an on-campus axe-murder story in the *New York Post*). The acts and omissions of the president's spouse, on the other hand, can harm *both* the college and herself. It is the seemingly contradictory roles of the spouse as apparent agent of the college and as one lacking in any real authority to act on behalf of the college that present the greatest danger to her—and the college.

Occasionally a president's spouse can be the recipient of community finger-wagging both because of her own actions *and* because of her apparent representation of the college. Again, Gordon and Constance Gee provide an example. In this instance, the usual elements of spouse criticism were arranged in an unusual order.

Very shortly after Gordon Gee became Chancellor of Vanderbilt University in 2000, his wife Constance was appointed Associate Professor of Public Policy and Education. As noted above, this was a tenured position. Her curriculum vitae which was posted on the Vanderbilt website described her teaching duties as follows: "I have taught *Public Policy, the Arts and Art*

Education for the Department of Leadership and Organizations and an introductory public policy course (HOD 2100) for the Human and Organizational Development Department . . ." [44] Thus, she was a presidential spouse with a relatively high campus profile.

In September 2006 a front-page article appeared in the *Wall Street Journal* under the headline, "Golden Touch: Vanderbilt Reins In Lavish Spending by Star Chancellor; As Schools Tighten Oversight, a $6 Million Renovation Draws Trustees' Scrutiny."[45] In an interesting twist on the usual dope-slapping of presidents' spouses for expenditures relating to the president's house, the *Journal* laid this "outrage" squarely at the feet of Gordon Gee—not at those of Constance Gee. It reported that Gordon Gee had spent more than $6,000,000 on renovations to the chancellor's residence, "Braeburn," and that the chancellor's entertainment expenses (including a full-time $50,000-per-year chef) topped $700,000 per year. Neither the renovation expense nor the entertainment expenditure had been approved by the full Vanderbilt Board.

Nonetheless, Constance Gee did not go unnoticed in the *Journal*'s report. The headline continued, "Marijuana at the Mansion."[46] In 2005 Constance Gee had been quietly reprimanded for possessing and using marijuana at "Braeburn." In a further tweaking of

---

[44] Constance Gee, Curriculum Vitae (see note 33 above).

[45] J. S. Lubin and D. Golden, *Wall Street Journal*, September 26, 2006, p. A1.

[46] Ibid.

campus sensibilities, Constance had lowered the flag at the chancellor's residence to half-staff following the 2004 election of George W. Bush and signed a public letter protesting Vanderbilt's recognition of National Security Advisor Condoleeza Rice as an appropriate recipient of the "Chancellor's Medal for Distinguished Public Service". Had Constance been almost any other faculty member, smoking a joint at home, lowering the flag at her residence to half-staff following "W's" election, and signing a "Condi Shouldn't Get the Medal" letter would not have caused much of a stir. However, because she was both a tenured faculty member *and* the wife of the chancellor, she was an easy target at which the *Wall Street Journal* could lob its anti–higher education artillery. The consequences of Constance's actions fell hard on both Vanderbilt and herself.

In 2012, Constance Gee published a book entitled *Higher Education: Marijuana at the Mansion,*[47] in which she recounted her experiences as a presidential spouse. She described various formative childhood experiences and the educational path which led her to meet, later marry, and ultimately divorce E. Gordon Gee.

As the title suggests, much of the text is given over to an explanation of the presence of marijuana at the Vanderbilt Chancellor's house. Constance provides a credible narrative, explaining that she suffered from Ménière's disease, a disorder of the inner ear which causes extreme vertigo and nausea. She had taken

---

[47] Constance B. Gee, *Higher Education: Marijuana at the Mansion* (Indianapolis, Ind.: Dog Ear Publishing, 2012).

various prescription drugs which had failed to ameliorate her symptoms and which had resulted in terrible side effects. She tried marijuana at the urging of a friend and found it effective in relieving the worst of her symptoms.

Constance stated that she had disclosed (in confidence) her use of marijuana to a member of the Braeburn staff. The confidence was not kept. The staff member's disclosure eventually reached the Vanderbilt board. This was just a final step in the descent of relations between Constance and some Vanderbilt employees. Other staff/university problems she experienced are set out above. After the marijuana discovery, Constance was essentially isolated by the university and by her husband. Eventually, she was left alone at Vanderbilt—without respect or a husband, but with tenure.

She later surrendered that tenure. In her memoir, *Higher Education: Marijuana at the Mansion*, Constance acknowledges that she left Vanderbilt but does not describe the terms under which she surrendered her tenured position. In her book, Constance reported that she was called to a meeting with her department chairman to discuss her plans vis-à-vis her teaching position, following E. Gordon's departure. When she declared her intention to remain in her tenured position, she alleged that the chairman urged her to leave Vanderbilt because others in the department "resented" her having been granted tenure and because "You [Constance] were forced down our throats." [48]

My attempts to obtain information on this subject from Vanderbilt legal counsel and from members of her

---

[48] Ibid., Chapter 25, "Endgames and New Beginnings."

department went unanswered. Similar inquiries about Constance's faculty position at Brown University were also rebuffed.

Interestingly, Constance does state unequivocally that while at both Vanderbilt and Brown, her best friends and most favored activities were located off campus—in East Nashville (Vanderbilt) and at the Providence art community (Brown). On the other side of the coin, her most strident and unforgiving critics were Brown and Vanderbilt university community members. Although her problems arose from different kinds of conduct from those described in later chapters of this book, the common denominator among them is university dislike of/antipathy to a presidential spouse seen to be exercising prerogatives which were not considered to be legitimately hers.

By her own description, Constance found consolation only when she left Vanderbilt and retreated first to East Nashville and later to her getaway house on the Westport, Massachusetts, beach—where, now, several years post-divorce, she is ready to move on with her life.

In reality, the spouse should be neither a Minister without Portfolio nor a trespassing interloper. The president's spouse is exactly that—the president's spouse. Her relevant relationship is with the president, not with the institution. When the spouse or the president loses sight of this reality, great mischief may follow. As long as the spouse is seen as acting as a private advisor to the president, she reveals no actions upon which criticism of her can be based. The spouse is a pure volunteer in service to her husband (as opposed to the college). The president is thus the intermediary between the spouse as volunteer and the college which is the indirect recipient of the value of that volunteering. I note parenthetically that it will be increasingly difficult for the president and his spouse to convey the real nature of such a relationship to the college as the spouse's participation in the affairs of the college becomes more obvious, intrusive, and apparently representative.

By clearly defining the spouse's status in a particular circumstance, the president is redefining the turf. To the extent that the president does so, he may become the object of the same criticisms to which his spouse was subject. However, the president has a job description which grants him the authority to make that decision. The spouse enjoys no such seal of authority and is ill-served and sometimes badly treated if she comes to believe that she has such authority. The wise presidential spouse functions better as a confidential counselor to the president than as a public extension of him.

The presidential spouse who distances herself from the business of the institution also runs risks. This is particularly true at colleges where the spouse's predecessor has been very active. Nonparticipation by the new spouse can and probably will be viewed as an expression of ingratitude or, worse still, disloyalty. In these circumstances the duty to relieve the spouse of unreasonable and counterproductive college community expectations falls urgently to the college's board of trustees. Adoption of a clear policy which mandates nonparticipation in supervisory relationships at the college will blunt campus criticism of the president's spouse—provided that the spouse honors the policy.

At still greater risk are the spouses of presidents of sectarian colleges where the model of the Minister's

Wife has a long pedigree. In these circumstances there are issues of religious doctrine which mix with the more mundane organizational complexities discussed above. Perhaps these spouses will not be relieved of their burdens short of the kind of litigation considered in Chapter 6.

Finally, the president's spouse must always ask herself why Dr. X or Mr. Y or Ms. Z is so very interested in her and/or her circumstances. In the vast majority of these situations, X, Y, and/or Z are genuinely interested and wholly benign. In a few situations, however, X or Y or Z will be trying to use a relationship with the spouse to influence the president. That person may be using the spouse to serve as a conduit for false information or mischaracterized information or defamatory information. In such situations it is best to keep the ears open and the mouth shut. The objective is to avoid a turf war—not to start one.

Ideally, the president's spouse should function, publicly, as a pure and *occasional* volunteer. If she works consciously to appear to be in charge of nothing, to cause the expenditure of zero college dollars, to have a life of her own, and nonetheless to be supportive of the president and the mission of the college, she can avoid contested turf and, like Caesar's wife, be beyond suspicion.

CHAPTER 4

AND IN YOUR NEW JOB YOU WILL REPORT TO . . .

At Ithaca College there is a guy I know in the Buildings and Grounds Department. I will call him "Sam." He likes boats. I like boats. He likes to work outside. I like to work outside. I think he is a great guy. He makes me feel that he thinks that I am a good guy. Notwithstanding all of our similarities, there is one point as to which we are completely different. He had to compete to get his job at the college, had to compete to achieve his position, and will have to compete to maintain or enhance his job status. He had to do positive things to get to where he is and to stay there.

I, on the other hand, did not compete for my role as the President's Spouse. I did not have to compete with other men to maintain or enhance my status as the husband of the President of Ithaca College. In connection with my role at Ithaca College, I did not have to do anything positive; I simply had to avoid doing anything which was seriously negative.

Although I am not familiar with any of its provisions, I know that Sam has a job description and that he will be held to perform his job in conformity with that job description. I know Sam's supervisor. He too is a great guy. And I am sure that he expects Sam to do his job and to do it well. If Sam does not do his job, his supervisor will call him to task. If Sam does not respond, he could lose his job or be subject to some other form of employee discipline.

I did not have a job description or a supervisor. If my wife were to assume the role of my supervisor, I would tell her where her authority ends with no fear of reprisal—at least as far as my role as presidential spouse is concerned. The only entity that could discharge me from my role as presidential spouse was a divorce court. The board of trustees, likewise, had no call on my time or my performance as presidential spouse; and if they did, they could only influence me through my wife. Sam and I were in very different places.

Sam is (among many other things) in charge of the building and grounds of the president's house. Although I sometimes lived in that house, I think it would have been extremely presumptuous of me to tell Sam how to mow the lawn or plow the driveway or fix the furnace (even though I think I knew how to do most of these things). These are not only areas of his expertise; they are his responsibility to his employer, the college. Were I to tell him how to do any of his jobs, I am sure he would be gracious—but sooner or later he would be asking himself and others, "Who does he think he is?" And the more I told him about how he should do his job, the sooner and more frequently and more publicly he would be asking that last question.

In my relations with college employees I tried very hard to avoid asking them to do things or telling them how to do the things they do. I did not always succeed in avoiding asking a favor of these employees, but I tried always to cast my request as a request—never as an order. I know about a housekeeper at another college who was so harangued by that president's spouse over the placement of knickknacks after dusting that she dusted with a ruler—measuring the exact location of the piece before dusting it so that it might be returned exactly to the spot from which it had been lifted. Clearly, that presidential spouse and I have very different styles.

Were this dusting-policing spouse to know of the disdain in which she was held by the housekeeping staff, I am sure she would feel hurt and betrayed. In her mind, she was just upholding proper standards for the dusting of a house and in return she was being disrespected by the staff. It seems to me that the tactful way around this problem would be for the president to talk to the housekeeper about standards. After all, it is his house. The staff can then gripe about the president, a part of whose job it is to be griped about.

A guy who really has this problem of authority/supervision scoped out is the Pope, because he never marries. By this simple omission, he avoids many of the problems encountered by college presidents, ministers, and their spouses. Minions he has, by the score, but no spouse.

Other clergy and college presidents do have something in common with the Pope. Their followers and constituents and the public in general tend to believe that they know a great deal more than they actually do. In the general uninformed view, the college president is selected because he knows what everybody else at the institution knows and at least a little bit more. This belief arises because some of the president's constituents want to believe that he is more-knowing if not all-knowing.

Most of the people who hire college presidents expect the president-elect to bring with him a spouse who will serve as a helpmate and who will, by the performance of good deeds for the college, facilitate the president's exercise of his vast intellect. Clergy who are permitted to marry also possess an aura of importance, based largely on the belief that they have a higher knowledge of, and likely access to, immortality. These clergymen's intense preoccupation with immortality leaves them insufficient time to deal with lesser, mundane matters, which are, in turn, left to their spouses. However, there are significant differences between the Pope's minions on the one hand and the president's or minster's wife on the other.

The Pope, clergy, and college presidents are subject to large amounts of public praise and private condemnation. Praise is given because the constituents have a need for leadership which appears to come from a higher, smarter, or otherwise superior place. Condemnation is given because the constituents tend to believe that their judgments are superior to their leaders' when it comes to issues relating to their individual job/life circumstances. Praise tends to be given publicly. Condemnation tends to be given out of earshot.

The faces which the Pope, college presidents, and clergy meet out in the world are usually open and friendly and are frequently complimentary. This is not to suggest that such indicia of deference are always genuine or sincere. A junior faculty member or a member of a congregation who, just a matter of minutes before meeting the college president or minister, was excoriating a recent decision of his/her leader, may become absolutely weak-kneed in the unexpected presence of that leader.

The Pope travels around the world bringing his message of faith and social policy to millions. Although many of those millions think fondly and approvingly of him every day, there are also many millions more who think little of him and would take to task, vigorously, many of his beliefs and the apparent consequences of those beliefs in the physical world. What nongovernmental organization (NGO) head would not covet the resources expended bringing the Pope to the many corners of the world he visits? Consider the cost of the Pope's retinue, the disruption of public services, and the cost of extra security—not to mention the transportation and maintenance of the Popemobile. Yet, bring that NGO head face-to-face with the Pope in Mexico City or Manila and there will be an apparent and instantaneous conversion. Unfortunately for the Pope, this conversion will probably be short-lived.

The same is true for the college president. Shortly after the face-to-face meeting, the junior faculty member who was glowing in her praise of the president's leadership will return to her fervent criticism of the repainting of the president's house. "Surely the money spent on the painting would have been better allocated to educational materials or faculty salaries."

Generally, however, because the college president has a spouse, he has an added disability which the Pope does not. When it comes time for painful allocation of limited resources, the very existence of that spouse becomes a liability for the president which does not appear on the Pope's institutional balance sheet. It is nearly impossible for a spouse to exist without some measure of expenditure of college funds being laid at her feet.

At a large majority of colleges there is a President's House. This house comes in many forms and in a vast variety of conditions. Some are well maintained by college staffs who take considerable pride both in the building and in their individual responsibilities for caring for the president's institutional needs. Others are buildings which, by reason of a tradition of deferred maintenance, or by reason of rough prior use or lack of funding, have simply fallen into disrepair.

No matter, when the temperature is very hot or very cold, some members of the academy, whose jobs, benefits, or other working conditions are in peril because of budget problems, will see thousands of dollars unnecessarily flying out the windows of the President's House in air conditioning or heating costs.

And why are these expenses necessary? The president is not in that house during the day . . . but the president's spouse or family may well be. The president may be throwing a development function at the house, but if the spouse is deeply involved in the planning and execution of what is perceived to be an expensive event, credit for the successful development component will usually flow to the president while blame for the expense will flow to the spouse.

Further, as any house expense becomes more discretionary (decoration as opposed to utilities), the potential for recrimination increases. To the extent that the president's spouse actually or apparently increases the expenses of the president's house, or any other college expense for that matter, she will present significant potential for the creation of campus discontent. This is particularly so in times of budgetary stress.

There is ever the tendency for the spouse to argue that the expenditures are necessary to enhance the development potential of the institution. Although this argument may or may not have legitimacy,[49] it frequently falls on unreceptive ears.

The Pope and his retinue are not exposed to these traps because the Pope does not have a spouse—and he makes sure that neither his close associates nor his junior faculty do either. In that way, much of the criticism to which the president's spouse is exposed is either avoided or, at worst, directed at someone who has a real and clearly understood place in the organization (in this instance, the church).

There are those who would criticize the Roman Catholic Church for its ownership of extremely valuable works of art and real estate. However, if Cardinal X is responsible for the expenditure of several hundreds of thousands of dollars in the restoration of a certain painting or church building and if some of the faithful are critical of his decision, at least the decision was made by a person clearly designated and authorized to make the decision.

If, ultimately, the decision turns out to be a very bad one, the Cardinal will have to answer to the Pope. Since the Cardinal's relationship to the Pope is considerably different from that of the spouse to the college president, the likelihood of transparency and accountability is much higher in the Cardinal's case than it is in the

---

[49] See Chapter 7, "Does She? Or Doesn't She? Only the Development Office Knows for Sure."

spouse's. The faithful of the church are far more likely to accept the Pope's defense or discipline of the Cardinal because the Pope/Cardinal relationship is organizational—not merely personal.

On the other hand, if the president's spouse is seen as having been responsible for a controversial expenditure of college money, the college community will not see the spouse as being clearly designated and authorized because the spouse is not seen as being accountable to anyone. In a private sense, the spouse is accountable to the president on a personal level. However, the college community will not see this as true accountability. The community will see the situation for what it is—nepotism. Put another way, the spouse will not likely be fired for a bad spending decision. This puts the spouse on a very different footing than any other employee of the college, and one not well received by many college communities. College publications, national higher education journals, and the public press are filled with stories of presidents whose tenures were shortened or made miserable by college community reaction to expenditures made (or perceived to have been made) by, or for the benefit of or at the behest of, the president's spouse.

Since the college president usually cannot obtain the Pope's advantage in these matters, it would be best for the presidential spouse to remove herself as far from the appearance of making or benefiting from the expenditure of college money as possible. Certainly, the spouse cannot turn the heat off in the president's house in winter, but she can limit her exposure to community censure by prudent management of those college resources which must (actually or apparently) pass through her hands.

It is noteworthy that some college employees will offer to provide goods and services to the spouse as a means of accommodating or impressing the president. Sometimes these offers are made in consummate good faith and sometimes they are made with Machiavellian intent. A respectful and thankful declining of such a favor can be much more valuable in the future than accepting such a favor in the present.

Intracollegiate public relations aside, the role played by the president's campus-engaged spouse raises basic ethical questions. Nepotism is defined as "favoritism shown to ... relatives because of their relationship rather than their merits."[50] I am hard pressed to distinguish the hiring of the president's spouse by a college into any position for which there was no competitive screening of candidates, from the foregoing definition of nepotism. And the nepotism label will attach to the spouse's situation whether or not she is paid. Even if the spouse is not paid, she probably will assume supervisory authority over college employees who must (actually or apparently) do the things which will effect her wishes. From the point of view of the supervisees and other third parties, the only rationale for the spouse's having such authority is her relationship to the president. This perception arises because her merit is not tested by other candidates. These third parties' skepticisms are ethically warranted.

---

[50] *Webster's Third New International Dictionary, unabridged* 1993 by Merriam-Webster, Incorporated (www.Merriam-Webster.com)

It is also true that many college communities learn, over time, that the president's spouse is, indeed, a competent, talented, and dedicated doer of college business. As a practical matter, community acceptance may be a solution to a particular nepotism problem. That reality does not, however, address the ethical issues arising from her noncompetitive empowering or hiring. When the mayor hires his brother to run the Street Department, the outcry is predictable—even if the brother does a good job with the streets.

For those inclined to criticize John F. Kennedy, the appointment of his brother Robert to be Attorney General was the equivalent of giving a French mob a pile of loose paving stones. The facts that the streets are well cared for and that Robert Kennedy did a great job with some very difficult circumstances do not erase the word *nepotism* from these appointments. Neither does the job performance of the appointed family member render an unethical appointment an ethical one.

In the best of circumstances, the definition of just what the president's spouse's role at the college is, is often vague and sometimes unknowable. However, actions can create apparent definitions. The more visibly the spouse acts in the college community or the more she is paid for her services, the clearer the community's definition of her role becomes—whether that definition is accurate or not.

At least one college system has been forced to confront these issues. The wife of the president of North Metro Technical College in Georgia had been employed in a counseling position at the college. A nepotism scandal at the Georgia Department of Technical and Adult Education had resulted in a revision of departmental regulations. Under these revisions, the president's spouse's arrangement at North Metro was considered to be in violation of the revised nepotism regulations. Since the president's spouse had been hired under the earlier regulations, there was no violation arising from the hiring. Only the *continuation* of her employment violated the new regulations. The North Metro president had to fire his wife.[51]

The gravamen of the complaint against nepotism is that the college is deprived of the potential fruits of a fair and competitive hiring process. A further complaint is that which argues that the hiring of the president's spouse presents an unacceptable potential for conflicts of interest.

The spouse who has no recognized role at the college her husband heads is not a stakeholder in any college constituency. If the Athletic Department gets more funding than the English Department thinks is appropriate, the spouse will not be publicly carrying the mail for either department. She may well have an opinion about the issue. If she does, the president will undoubtedly hear about it. But the public will, in the usual circumstance, have absolutely no knowledge of her position. She has influence with the president but is not accountable to either the English or the Athletic Department.

Let's assume, however, that upon the president's selection by the board, he announced that his wife deserved an appointment in the English Department and

---

[51] S. Jaschik, "President Forced to Fire His Wife," *Inside Higher Ed*, June 13, 2005, http://www.insidehighered.com/news/2005/06/13/nepotism(accessed March 13, 2013).

that absent such an appointment the president-designate could not accept the presidency. Dutifully, a vacancy was created and the president's highly qualified spouse became part of the English Department. Setting aside the discontent of those who would have liked to compete with the spouse for that seat, can we postulate a conflict-of-interest scenario?

How about this? In the next budget cycle, all of the departments of the college have developed proposed budgets and submitted them to the provost and the treasurer. Unfortunately for the English Department, a personal rift has developed between the provost and the chairman of the English Department. When the final budget numbers are crunched into a proposal to the board, the English Department perceives itself as having taken a major hit.

The president is vaguely aware of the personal problems between the provost and the chairman of the English Department but does not see any connection between the budget numbers and internecine ill will. He is aware of his own need for a positive and close relationship with his provost and has frequently told his wife how heavily he relies on his provost and how difficult it would be to replace him. The budget will be acted upon by the board in the very near future.

To whom does the president's spouse owe her highest loyalty? Is it to her department, her students, her colleagues, the college, or her husband? If she is firmly of the opinion that the provost is just being a mean-spirited jerk who is acting out of ill-considered and vindictive motives, should she bring this to the attention of her husband, the president? Surely, if she is acting on behalf of the department, students, colleagues, or college, the answer is an unequivocal "yes." At the same time, she knows that should she raise these issues with her husband, she may well destroy the very important relationship between her husband and the provost. Casting a further shadow over this scene is the fact that the spouse has a financial and/or professional interest in the outcome of the budget approval process.

If the spouse says nothing to the president and the unfair budget goes through, not only will her students suffer, she will suffer financial or professional consequences as well. If she engages with her husband on the level of pillow talk, the president/provost relationship is threatened. And if she goes public with what she knows (or thinks she knows), it will probably embarrass her husband, herself, and the board.

What should she do? I propose she climb into a time machine, dial back to the day before she was appointed to the English Department, put the thing in reverse, and, on arrival, take up some other work.

CHAPTER 5

JOBS, ROLES, MONEY . . . DO NOT MIX

Everyone expects the pastor to pass the collection plate once or twice and to tell the congregation that there are great needs in the world which must be met. However, when the pastor's wife shows up the following week with a new coat and new shoes, it does not matter that these items were (really) gifts from her mother. That's just not the way the congregation is going to sense it. Mixing mission and spouses is not good medicine. Adding money, or the appearance of money, can make things worse.

There are relatively few jobs for which the employer makes substantial demands and the employee receives no material compensation—and women seem to hold most of these kinds of jobs. From the housewife to the nun to the child-care provider to the college president's wife, the rationales for these seemingly unjust arrangements have common themes. She is being given a living situation (be that living marginal or substantial), and in return the least she can do is earn her keep.

Although I would like to believe that such thinking is obsolete, it holds substantial currency with higher education boards today. The male president's female spouse is most often expected to maintain the president's house in a manner suitable for entertaining (sometimes with and sometimes without a budget); to travel with the president whenever the board thinks it might be advantageous to the college for her to do so; to do such child rearing as is necessary, provided always that the children never interfere with the efficient operation of the college; to be gracious, attractive, and coyly witty in service to any development situation into which she may (voluntarily or involuntarily) be thrust; to serve as both an ambassador to and a spy on faculty spouses (roles frequently conjoined in international relations); to perform such other duties as may be assigned; and to do all of these things without expressing a thought of substantial complexity or otherwise showing up her betters.

Usually, this president's spouse is compensated for all of these good deeds by having the privilege of living in The President's House (often, at best, a mixed blessing); enduring a travel schedule which substantially interferes with her job, child rearing, and all other normal activities; eating food which is not healthy; and getting kicked around by campus malcontents of every stripe. In addition she often has to pass not-so-subtle inspections by the wives of board members and of other self-proclaimed stakeholders in the college and the surrounding community. These inspections take place on and off the campus.

I recall a presidential spouse lamenting that she had to police her young adult son who used to wash his car on Sunday while wearing cut-off jeans—not in the church parking lot, but in the driveway behind the president's house. "The community was offended," she was told. She had to wear a skirt or dress while picking up a gallon of milk at the nearby 7-11 because she had been told that wearing shorts, slacks, or jeans on such an errand just wasn't done. As a kid, I knew girls who went to Catholic schools where the dress codes were more relaxed than the ones this poor woman had to obey. And for all of this she was paid . . . nothing.

The unfairness of this situation arises because the spouse thinks of what she is doing as a *job* while the board thinks of what she is expected to do as her *role*. It is important to distinguish jobs from roles. Former Secretary of State Hillary Rodham Clinton observed that leaving the White House and taking on her own political life had not caused her to feel liberated. Rather she said, "I wouldn't use that (word) . . . You know, before Bill ran for president, I had my own job . . . There's nothing comparable to being First Lady. It's not a *job*; it's a *role* . . . (emphasis added)."[52] Abner Mikva, a Democratic former U.S. Representative, federal judge, law professor from Chicago, and longtime friend of Barack and Michelle Obama, provides this description of a political wife: "Being a political wife is not the greatest job in the world. Your ego is stomped on, and you're pushed aside, and you're always the senator's wife, the congressman's wife, the state legislator's wife [the college president's wife]—you're never a person in your own being . . . (your) social engagements have to be made through . . . campaign staff. There's good cause for resentment."[53] What Mikva describes is a role, although he mislabels it as a job. In twenty-first-century America, people are compensated for performing jobs. They are not paid for fulfilling roles. Hillary Clinton was not paid for her role as the First Lady, but she

---

[52] Elizabeth Kolbert, "The Student," *New Yorker*, October 13, 2003, p. 72. Acknowledged to be "fair use" by the author.

[53] Abner Mikva, interview by Liza Mundy, in *Michelle: A Biography* (New York: Simon & Schuster, 2008), pp. 128–129. Used by permission of Abner Mikva.

certainly has been compensated for her job as a United States Secretary of State.

However, anyone with normally functioning senses should be able to perceive that the president's spouse's role is to do a lot of work; and if she's doing all this work, it is fair to argue that she should be paid for it.

A troublemaking wag might question, "If Michelle Obama is not being paid to fulfill her role as First Lady, why should the First Lady of XYZ University be paid for her role? Both involve a great deal of work, with Michelle Obama probably doing more of it than the spouse of the president of XYZ University." I would argue that Michelle Obama will have a much greater opportunity to be compensated for her efforts after leaving office than will the XYZ U spouse; and that Michelle and Barack Obama's service was to a political community of the whole (i.e. public service) and as such is different qualitatively from service to a single university.

No matter how that argument is resolved, I cannot re-read the beginning of this chapter without feeling that a great injustice is being done to female college presidential spouses in the circumstances I describe. A simple remedy for this injustice might be to pay spouses for the work they do on behalf of the college. Payment of compensation to spouses is often discussed and is finding acceptance in an increasing number of institutions.

The urge to compensate the spouse comes from at least three sources: First is institutional guilt caused by the college's dawning awareness that its treatment of presidents' spouses, by modern standards, has been shabby—at best. Second is advocacy by presidents and their spouses: Lengthy enumerations of the number of college events planned, executed, and attended by the president's spouse are made both as a part of advocacy for spouse compensation and as defenses against allegations of extravagance. Although the latter get a lot more public attention, the former is probably more frequently utilized. Third is the influence of the Internal Revenue Service. This source is troublesome because while the first two sources of momentum toward spouse compensation may have some grounding in educational purposes, the IRS source does not.

Until fairly recently times, Mrs. or Ms. President's Spouse could tag along with the president for development trips and throw development events at the president's house without having to look over her shoulder or in the flower arrangement for an IRS agent or an IRS microphone. However, inspired by the federal government's recent, broad-based hostility toward higher education, and buoyed by some extremely extravagant abuses by a few college administrations, the IRS has made the traditional activities of presidents' spouses into tax traps. If Mrs. President's Spouse joins her husband on a capital campaign trip to Singapore (or Elizabeth, N.J.), the college's reimbursement of her travel expenses could become taxable income to her.

This would not necessarily be a bad thing, if it motivated spouses to step away from the traditional roles to which they have been indentured. Instead, the buzz at CIC and AASCU has centered on how the spouse can become an employee of the college. As employees doing their college's work, reimbursement of their expenses is not income to them and continues to be (in for-profit institutions) a deduction for the college.

No matter what the impetus may be for employing and paying the spouse, rank-and-file college employees (especially those supervised by the spouse) may view the spouse as enjoying special and favored status based solely on her being the president's wife. From the employees' standpoint this special treatment is hard enough to take if the spouse is a volunteer. It is more difficult to swallow if the president's spouse is being paid for her role/job.

Unfortunately, the necessary consequences of this employ-and-pay solution are sometimes more corrosive to the fabric of the college community and to the psyche of the spouse than the injustice of the spouse's exploitation as a so-called volunteer.

Here is a real-life example. Names of the players and the playgrounds have been changed. In the near past, Frothingschloss (fictional name) University engaged KM as its new president. President M had served with considerable distinction as dean of a very prestigious professional school at another top-tier university before moving to the Frothingschloss University presidency. Shortly after assuming his duties, his wife began to appear at meetings in the president's office and to participate actively in those meetings.

Many persons invited to meet with President M were surprised and a little put off by his wife's presence and participation. Later it developed that the Frothingschloss University board had engaged M's wife as a "special advisor" to the university. She reported directly to the board. Thus, the organizational chart had two lines running to the university board of trustees—one for M and a separate one for his wife. She was compensated with a five-figure salary by the board for her services.

M's wife, AB, had a substantial background in higher education development and was quite familiar with some aspects of the affairs of large universities, having come to Frothingschloss from a high-level development position at another top-tier university. Although there was little criticism of Ms. AB's background, there was a general unease in the campus community resulting from her open participation in top-level decision making and because she was being paid. In this context it was hard to determine if she was fulfilling a role or doing a job.

I submit that much of that campus feeling derived from the fact that, like me, Ms. AB had not competed for her job and was not supervised in any meaningful way by the board of trustees. She enjoyed a position of considerable public influence over the affairs of Frothingschloss U, not because she had been selected as the cream of some search crop, but because she was married to the president.

Further, her influence extended far beyond the range of her current expertise. In that environment it mattered little whether her influence was brilliant or dull or bad; it just didn't feel right. The salary check did not make things one bit better.

Conversations in the community reflected that feeling. Although the vast majority of members of the Frothingschloss community seemed to genuinely like President M and his wife, her participation combined with her compensation by the university left many resentful of the arrangement (if not of the individuals). It just was not a good idea.

Frothingschloss had left itself open to a further problem, which thankfully did not materialize. Having hired Ms. AB, purportedly on her own merits, what would happen if President M stepped down? Ironically, that is exactly what happened. Had Ms. AB decided to stay on in her job, on what basis could the board cause her to vacate that job? If she was serving with distinction, there would be no *cause* for which she could be removed. If she was moved out because her husband had resigned, was she being discharged because she was married to M (and thus fired because of her marital status)? If she served "at the pleasure of the board," what were the board's true motives in asking or ordering her to leave? What were the sources of the board's displeasure? In any of these cases the university could have had serious legal and/or public-relations problems on its hands.

At another college, the president's spouse was designated by the board as Special Assistant to the President. The board provided this spouse with a Position Description and a Letter of Agreement which provided that she would report to the board. The Letter of Agreement stated, in no uncertain terms, that the spouse would continue doing exactly what she had been doing; only she would be paid for it.

The board did not undertake to seriously superintend her work, describing her work as "autonomous." This spouse's report to the board consisted of two-plus typewritten pages reciting the number of college events planned, hosted, and/or attended, community organizations joined, and trips made in the interests of the college. The true significance of this document was its attempt to immunize the spouse from IRS scrutiny— not to serve the college. There was no suggestion in any of the paperwork that anyone but the president's spouse could ever qualify for the position of Special Assistant to the President.

Not long ago, I attended a higher education institute at which Spouse Workshops were offered. One session was entitled "Working on the Campus at Which Your Spouse Is President." Joining me at a breakout session table were four (4) women spouses of male presidents.

One of the women had been employed as an administrator by her college before she married the president. The second was employed part-time in the library of her college. The third held a full-time teaching position at her college. The fourth became a full-time college volunteer upon her husband's hiring and was considering seeking regular employment at her college. I was the final participant.

Initially, the conversation concerned the various firewalls which had been erected at each college to create the impression that the spouse was receiving no special consideration by reason of her relationship with the president. None of the women reported directly to her husband/president. One woman believed that her status as a college employee prior to her marriage would immunize her from nepotism concerns or other forms of discrimination. She did not feel that future decisions concerning her status with the college would be affected by her marital situation.

There was unanimity among the women that they were required to work harder and longer to demonstrate the absence of any special status which derived from their marriages to their respective husband/presidents. All of the women initially cited their long service as evidence of the appropriateness of their employment and of their acceptance by the college community.

As the conversation progressed, however, each of the women related one or more incidents which had made her and/or her president/spouse feel awkward because of the circumstances of her campus employment. Nonetheless, all of the women held to the belief that the problems which they had encountered were, by and large, incidental and manageable.

Still later in the conversation, I asked whether, as a general proposition, spouses could be employed on campus, given proper preparations and firewalls. I also asked if they felt it was fair that they were expected to work longer and harder to avoid the pall of suspected nepotism. On this point there was a consensus of the women that the heightened expectations were real and were not fair. Nonetheless these women uniformly believed that they were being discriminated against, but that this just came with the territory.

I then related a number of incidents in which I had told board members and other college community members that I considered my loyalty and responsibility was to my wife, not to the college. The women unanimously responded that "a woman would never get away with that."

Generally speaking, the women were right. The easy assumption has been that a woman will serve the college without clear guidance or any compensation. Colleges get away with this exploitation largely because no one in the system wants to rock the boat. Why does it appear that so many women and so few men are willing to be exploited in this way? Who should blow the whistle on these practices?

The least likely whistle-blowers would seem to be those spouses (male and female) whose business, professional, or academic status immunizes them from institutional demands. They have escaped the "volunteered" trap and have no particular motivation to create a controversy.

Male spouses, who have generally continued to pursue their professions and interests away from the college, are not motivated to protest. Their lack of interest in these issues may derive from the fact that male board members (who predominate) are much more accepting of a male spouse pursuing a career not related to college service than of a woman doing the same thing.

Thus, it is left to the women who have traditionally been exploited, who made the sacrifice to see their husbands become presidents, and those spouses who live for the experience of feeling queenly, to make some noise. Unfortunately, these folks are not terribly likely to advocate their own abdication (even if it is an abdication of a position which is unfair or even dangerous to them).

To bridge the gap between the president's spouse's responsibilities as a volunteer and her apparent lack of institutional status/authority, the modern spouse argues that there is no better way to ameliorate this problem than by rubbing some cash on her situation. The problem with this approach is that, as stated above, the solution creates two problems harder to solve than the initial ones.

The two problems are: 1) campus discomfort (and sometimes hostility) because the spouse is holding a job for which there was no competition/supervision; and 2) the possible legal consequences of trying to get rid of the spouse in any number of hypothetical situations. Both problems are aggravated if the spouse is being paid for her services.

There is a way around these problems. The board should not permit the hiring of the president's spouse to any college position without a genuinely open and public search. With very few exceptions, the board should make it clear that the spouse will have no responsibilities to or authority over the college or any of its employees. The board should encourage him or her to continue with whatever he or she was doing before the engagement of the president, be that neurosurgery or homemaking. The board should try in any reasonable way to help the spouse secure desired employment or engagement in the community outside the college, and make that spouse a welcome member of the college community and the larger community beyond the college.

The problems of hiring presidential spouses are distinguishable from the problems of hiring trailing spouses. If XYZ College wants to obtain the professional services of Professor Grande, and if Professor Grande is indeed grand, the college will probably find itself in competition with other colleges and universities for his services. In the rough and tumble of the competition for Grande's services, it is not uncommon for Grande to point out that Ms./Dr. Grande is a gifted and talented academic and that one Grande does not move without the other Grande. The scramble is then on to find a position for Ms./Dr. Grande. The winner of Professor Grande's services may well be the one which finds the best situation for Ms./Dr. Grande.

This is all part and parcel of current recruiting and job-seeking practices. However, the Grande hypothetical is distinguishable from the president/president's spouse hire in several respects. First, Ms./Dr. Grande will not report to Professor Grande. Ms./Dr. Grande will have a real job description, will be subject to regular performance reviews by her supervisors, and may suffer disciplinary consequences for material professional errors or omissions. Unless she is hired into a tenured position, her path to tenure will be the same as that of all other tenure aspirants. Both Ms./Dr. Grande and the college community will understand that in these circumstances, the limitations set out above are real. The person or persons who were displaced by Ms./Dr. Grande's employment will probably be unhappy, but the institutional discontent will not likely spread beyond this small group.

In the case of the president's spouse, all of the features of the typical trailing-spouse hire which make it acceptable to the college community are absent. To the extent that the president's spouse reports to anyone, she will report to her husband or the board. Her job description, if one exists, will not be meaningful and she will not be subject to real job performance review or discipline. The more the president's spouse exercises her supposed authority, the sooner the college community will come to view her as having special and unearned status. The cases of the professor's wife and the president's spouse are very different.

CHAPTER 6

TRUTH . . . OR CONSEQUENCES

The two boards of trustees to whom my wife reported understood issues of expectations (or rather non-expectations) of their presidents' spouses. However, there are many, many boards and trustees who have never invested time in a serious consideration of the ethical and legal ramifications of continuing business as usual as it relates to the president's spouse and the college's expectations of her. This chapter is intended to explore some of the blind spots and some of the perils awaiting the board which continues to believe that in hiring a president, it got two for one.

When I assert that presidential spouses owe no duty to the college, the first response is, "But what if the spouse, and the college she serves, like the role of the traditional presidential spouse?" This response was recently cast in a slightly different light by my sister-in-law. She is married to a very successful investment analyst and has done the good-corporate-wife-thing for decades. She opined that the trouble with my thesis was that the good wife, having put her husband through college (and/or graduate school) and raised the kids pretty much alone (and in the shadow of undergraduate misbehaviors) and attended and/or hosted all of those boring college social events and put up with the loneliness of it all, should have a chance to strut her stuff at college expense. She's earned it.

My rejoinder (ignoring for the moment the petty naggings of the IRS) is that the proper person to show appreciation for her sacrifice is her husband, not the college. Although the college may have benefited from her acts and sacrifices, she did it for him—not for it. The flowers and candy should come from hubby, not from the bursar's office. When a president gets into trouble, investigative reporters almost always dig into records of funds expended by, for, or at the direction of the president's spouse. The president of American University, Benjamin Ladner, came under fire in 2005 for his expenditure of university funds. Although Ladner sought to justify expenditures which appeared to benefit his wife by citing some 240 university-related events which she had attended in a single year, the *Washington Post* reported, "Nancy Ladner's time that was documented in chauffeur's logs and the social secretary's calendar includes frequent trips to a salon, jewelry shops and engagements on Gibson Island, where they have a weekend home."[54] And further, "Ladner said most of the thousands of dollars that his wife charged to AU for household furnishings, food and beverages and that was questioned by the companies hired to do the audit was consistent with the terms of his contract."[55]

Whether the money was spent for her or at her behest and whether the work she did for the university

[54] S. Kinzie and V. Strauss, "AU's Ladner Defends His Spending," *Washington Post*, September 24, 2005, p. B4.

[55] Ibid., p. B1.

was worth the amount of the alleged expenditures are really beside the point. The mere fact of Ms. Ladner's participation as an apparent spender of university funds and the resulting circumstance that her name could be attached to particular expenditures gave rise to troubling issues which could have been avoided by her leaving no actual or implied fingerprints on college money. At the end of the story, *President* Ladner was on the public relations hook for what *Ms.* Ladner spent.

A senior college administrator of my acquaintance suggested that the arguments of this piece must admit exceptions for those spouses, like the wife of the president of his institution, who really loved to perform the traditional role of the presidential spouse. It is an interesting geographical aside that the college where he works is located in a region where traditions (such as the notion of the antebellum spouse) die hard.

The administrator of whom I speak is a fair, open-minded, and thoughtful person. In his view, the president's spouse at his college was very happy in her role and was very effective in communicating with college staff. The instrument of communication which he mentioned most frequently was the freshly baked cookie. I could not help framing a mental picture of a woman clad in hoop skirts with auburn curls cascading from beneath a piece of nineteenth-century millinery. In my mind's eye, she was swishing up a short stairway to an open door. In the doorway stood a somewhat shorter, obviously younger woman who was similarly attired. The younger woman held her hands clasped below her chin, her head tilted ever so slightly to the right, her eyes rolled upward toward the sky. She appeared to be about to receive some form of communion, if not a direct communication from some higher power. The older, auburn-haired woman carried a basket on her left arm. Although the contents of the basket were indistinct, they were obviously nestled in a white napkin. The woman's right hand was extended toward the younger woman, very much like Michelangelo's *The Creation of Adam*, and in that hand was a freshly baked chocolate chip cookie.

While this may be the way the president's spouse is viewed on that campus, when other traditional presidential spouses show up for spouse seminars at higher education conferences, they paint a very different picture. This picture looks a lot more like Cinderella in her pre-prince days—with lots of dirty dishes, floors in need of scrubbing, a wardrobe taken directly from *Les Misérables*, and an attitude born of a sense of institutional exploitation and ingratitude.

Surely, there are presidential spouses who are truly happy in their traditional roles and will continue to serve nobly and effectively. However, being happy and effective today does not mean one will necessarily be happy and effective tomorrow. How does one articulate the boundary which seems to separate the happy traditional spouse from the bitter and exploited one? Any college would be delighted to have a happy traditional spouse as opposed to one who thinks she is being exploited. If a board of trustees could discern and define the boundary between those two states of being and implement policies which clarify that boundary, the president, the spouse, and the institution would all be much better off.

In some instances the spouse is truly motivated by dedication to the institution and will do good deeds without need of any expression of appreciation or the receipt of any kind of compensation. I think the number of such spouses is tiny. The larger number of happy spouses consists of those who do their good deeds because of their relationship with their president/spouse—not their relationship with the college. From where I stand, it is much easier to endure (and even to enjoy) a development dinner if attending that event is viewed as giving me time together with my wife, partaking of the company of friends. Some would rejoin that such dinners are places where dull and tedious persons abound. However, before the ascendancy of the president, he and his wife socialized with groups of people, some of whom were enlightened and entertaining and some of whom were profoundly boring or worse. The same mix of people will be found at the development event. If the spouse is there because the college makes her go, generally she will do her duty; but without some personal benefit, she will, sooner or later, grow resentful. After all, she is doing all of this work and receiving neither financial compensation nor clearly expressed appreciation.

The most credible source of clearly expressed appreciation is the president. If the spouse participates because of her understanding with her husband and receives reinforcement in this enterprise from him, it is less likely that she will feel taken advantage of by the institution. In a situation where the spouse is constructively supporting the president, the board should find ways of encouraging the spouse without entangling her in the internal affairs of the college. On the other hand, although some representatives of the college may provide positive feedback, there are always campus curmudgeons whose crotchety voices seem to drown out the more helpful ones. If the college has no call on the spouse's time and presence save that to which she and the president agree, the curmudgeon is left howling in the wilderness.

Although some spouses follow the traditional behaviors because they really like the work, many more, I suspect, do so because of inertia. It is simply easier to go along with the institutional expectations than to try to buck them. There are many rationalizations for following this course of action.

During the presidential search process, spouses know that there are many aspirants to the presidency, but only one winner. If the aspirant and his spouse are involved in a close and loving relationship, you can bet that the spouse will do whatever she can do, reasonably, to advance the cause of her husband. If the spouse is interviewed, directly or indirectly, she will probably try to tease out the details of her predecessor spouse's profile on campus. If that profile is positive, the spouse will naturally try to demonstrate her ability and inclination to perform similarly. If it is negative, the spouse will try to distinguish herself from that profile. It is the least she can do to advance the candidacy of her husband. Unfortunately, such accommodation (which is the product of the immense power imbalance between the spouse and the board/search committee) sows the seeds of later discontent.

Even if the spouse declares her independence during the search process, once the president is enshrined (notwithstanding the spouse's pre-enshrinement candor about her non-role) the institution will make demands. These demands are hard to ignore—as stated earlier

(Chapter 3, "Why Do They Hate Me?—Turf Wars"). These will usually involve someone pointing the spouse on to someone else's turf.

But no matter what the demand or suggestion, the urge to perform will be hard to resist. The college is built on a foundation of loyalty. Even if you do not memorize the lyrics of the alma mater[56] you know roughly what they say. The college is our "fostering mother." Whatever you were supposed to do and refrain from doing with respect to your mother goes twice for dear old alma mater. How can a spouse ignore Mom's needs?

The answer is simple: The college is not your mother and the person enticing the spouse into some college-related activity is not Mom's agent. If the spouse takes on cookie baking because she and the president agree that this will be a good thing, it probably will be a good thing—provided that the president and the spouse are very honest with each other in the making of these decisions. Otherwise, the spouse should do something else.

In conversation with a former college president who is currently a search consultant, I was assured most earnestly that in certain regions of America, there is a long tradition of heavy institutional reliance on the president's spouse. In those circumstances, he assured me, the presidential spouse was entitled to compensation.

---

[56] Learning the alma mater will gain the spouse an immense store of institutional good will—particularly if the spouse knows more verses than the board does.

Let's put that assertion to a basic sniff test. If a college which was attempting to hire a new president tried to run the following draft position announcement, do we think it would make it through the legal department and into the *Chronicle of Higher Education*?

Northwest Southeast College at Regret
President
The college solicits nominations for the office of President. Doctorate and a strong background in development and personnel relations are required. The successful candidate must also have a spouse with demonstrated experience in managing a large house, entertaining, and other development activities. Spouse must have an outgoing personality and be attractive. Compensation of the President will be commensurate with his qualifications.

Application deadline: January 1, 2009
Reply to: Presidential Search Committee
Northeast Southwest College
Regret, Confusion 99999.

If a college would not dare advertise in this manner, on what ethical grounds does that same college anticipate and ultimately demand the services of the president's spouse? If the college really expects such spouse services, paid or unpaid, should it not further state in its solicitation, "Unmarried persons need not apply" or "Candidates with unattractive or introverted spouses need not apply" or "Gay candidates need not apply" or "Candidates with shaky marriages or uppity, independent wives need not apply"?

Often the ethical correctness of what one does in private can be tested by considering whether or not one would do the same thing in public. Translated to this context, would a college dare to openly demand services from a candidate's spouse which heretofore it only privately expected? I think not–with the possible exception of the University of Alabama which so burdened its new president's spouse with social (i.e. development) obligations that the new president resigned after 58 days on the job to protect his wife's health.[57]

Another test of the hiring of "two for one" (the unpaid spouse) or "one for one and another for a little more" (the compensated spouse) examines the ethical and emotional legitimacy of such hires as seen from the perspectives of the college and the spouse.

The college's view of the ethics of expecting the president's spouse to serve in an institutional role: The college cannot view such an expectation to be ethically valid because it would not dare to advertise its true intentions/expectations. Additionally, minimum wage, unemployment, and workers' compensation laws, as well as antidiscrimination laws (individually or collectively), would prohibit a college from acting on its traditional expectation of an unpaid presidential spouse. Minimum wage, unemployment, and workers' compensation laws would also prohibit engaging the spouse with compensation for the reasons set out in the next paragraph. Antidiscrimination laws would prohibit the college from requiring that the president have a

---

[57] *Women in Higher Education,* February 2013, p. 3

spouse. No matter how the college dresses this concept up, the clothes are transparent and the conduct is unethical and/or unlawful.

The spouse's view of the ethics of expecting her to serve in an institutional role: The spouse also knows that being hired to work for nothing is not an ethical thing for a college to anticipate. Even if she is hired with an understanding that she will be paid some sort of a stipend, that stipend will not vaguely pay her the worth of her services. Payments to her will also increase the potential for institutional hostility. The reality and the potential are both bad here.

The college's emotional desires relating to the president's spouse: If colleges have one attribute which comes all the way from their medieval origins, it is respect for and adherence to tradition. Colleges which have a tradition of active institutional involvement by the president's spouse feel a need to continue that tradition. It's in the institutional DNA. In the typical situation, the spouse serves as entertainer, hostess, and campus mother. It feels good. It feels right. Emotionally, this is a no-brainer: the college wants and needs its presidential spouse.

The spouse's emotional desires relating to the role of presidential spouse: This is a bit more complicated. For the spouse who has previously served as a Presidential Spouse, the role is well known[58]—and privately, at least, not very much appreciated. The role is assumed by her (again) in order to help the president get into another presidency. It is an act of consummate love.

---

[58] Even if the local politics are not.

The first-time president's spouse generally has little real knowledge of what she is getting into. From the outside, the role looks somewhat important and at least a little scary. Once the role is assumed, however, the differences in emotional satisfaction between new and experienced practitioners of the presidential spouse's arts disappear.

There is a group of presidential spouses who do not fit conveniently into the two categories set out above. These are the *queenly*[59] spouses—spouses who are energized by their role and expect/demand homage from their subjects. Superficially, they would seem to be emotionally fulfilled. However, the spouse who expressed the *queenly* feeling concept, Jean Kemeny, sometimes described herself as being angry, offended, and underappreciated. Most presidential spouses seem to be more emotionally content before and after their service to their various colleges and much less so while on duty. Few of these spouses are emotionally served or supported by their roles as presidential spouses.

Summing up these four considerations, there is a three-to-one majority against the traditional model of the college president's spouse. Only the college's emotional need for one of its traditions prevents the condemnation of this role from being unanimous.

Finally, doing the traditional-spouse-thing because of inertia dooms the spouse's successor to the same fate. No one outside sectarian institutions will maintain that two for one is fair or admit that it is practiced at their school. Nonetheless, it is happening at the majority of colleges and universities in America. Until these

[59] See Chapter 1, "I Get No Respect."

educational communities start trying to honestly answer the "what if we changed our expectations of the president's spouse" questions, and to act on the reasonable answers to those questions, the unfairness (and unhappiness) will continue.

And another example . . . The spouse of a college president in New England gained considerable notoriety by regularly chasing students and community members out of the college orchard. In the spouse's mind she was performing a valuable protective service. Unfortunately, there had been a long tradition of students and others filching a few pieces of fruit from the orchard—a tradition which substantially predated this particular presidential spouse's tenure.

In the student and the general-public communities, the president's spouse's reputation morphed into a caricature. Stories abounded about this Fury-like creature which, with arms waving and a voice like thunder, drove the sinners from the Eden of the college's orchard. Dark tales which were entirely lacking in any factual foundation circulated. The community disrespected the spouse and, as often happens, the disrespect was reciprocated. Everyone was pretty miserable until the president and the spouse moved on to other pursuits. Surely, the old tales are occasionally retold in the college community, and just as surely, the spouse must, from time to time, feel the pangs of dedication and altruism scorned.

This unhappy set of circumstances could have been avoided. The spouse could have taken more care to learn the traditions or habits of the college before arrogating to herself the job of orchard security. By the same token, representatives of the college, recognizing the public relations peril to which the spouse was exposed, could have clued her in. Unfortunately, the culture of the campus sometimes militates against this simple, curative exchange of information. The communication gap arises because of the unique status of the spouse. She is neither employee nor volunteer—neither fish nor fowl. She appears to be important but she really is not. If the campus culture is not going to educate the spouse, the spouse had best try to avoid taking on any institutional role. The first rule of medical ethics applies: "First, do no harm."

Even if the ethical issues raised above can be ignored, there are legal issues to be considered. If boards, presidents, spouses, and others involved in presidential searches do not reform their ways of thinking about the role/job of the presidential spouse, litigation may follow. Included in Appendices B and C are legal complaints arising from one fictional presidential search. They are intended to illustrate some of the hazards which boards and search committees face when considering the role of a candidate's spouse or a president's spouse.

The first hypothetical suit is brought by George and Gerri Knot. He was a candidate for President of Northeast Southwest College, whose candidacy was derailed because his wife could not fulfill the traditional role as the college's first lady. The second suit is brought by Cube Root, the spouse of the successful presidential candidate. She asserts that she was misled in the search process—being told that there were no particular expectations of her as a presidential spouse, when the college had major, unstated expectations which she had been forced to try to perform. Both plaintiffs seek compensatory and punitive damages.

There are good and sufficient reasons why boards and search committees should not inquire into the marital status of presidential candidates. Almost everyone involved in presidential searches knows not to ask "one of those questions." However, there are slightly more subtle ways of asking that question which are almost universally employed. A direct interview of the spouse of the candidate is the most obvious. Another is the social invitation. Another is a tour of the president's house.

Search committees' beliefs that a presidential candidate's spouse is a potential source of advantage or disaster has had currency for a long time. F. W. Neiss, in an Association of Governing Boards *Report*, argued that "It is sheer folly for the committee not to bring (the presidential candidate's) wife out as well. In a survey a few years back only one out of 140 new male college presidents, other than members of the priesthood, was unwed . . . The first lady plays so focal a role both at home and on campus that to exclude her from the screening process is to court probable disaster. Of course it is expensive to bring her along, but it can be far more expensive to leave her at home."[60]

All of these devices enable the board or the search committee to employ what I call the "three-eye" or "six-finger" test. Get the spouse into some setting where the committee or board representative can count to be sure that the candidate's spouse has (metaphorically) not

[60] F. W. Neiss, "The Recruitment and Retention of Presidents," *AGB Reports* 13 (1970): 10.

more than two eyes and not more than five fingers (per hand). The desire of the board or search committee to have this kind of information is nearly irresistible because institutional tradition creates an expectation that the presidential spouse will perform highly public (and usually unpaid) work for the college and the board had best find out, in advance, if she is cut out for it. The more subtle means of obtaining this information are at present considered innocuous.

In applying the three-eye or six-finger test, a board may be asking one of two questions. The first is, "Will the spouse's appearance or behavior significantly detract from the candidate's performance of his duties as president?"[61] The second is, "Is the spouse 'up to' the role or job of presidential spouse?" The first question is legitimate, *provided* that the basis for answering this question in the negative is not rooted in some form of unlawful discrimination.[62] The second question is never legitimate.

Unfortunately, there is always the lawsuit from hell awaiting an opportunity. The complaint in *George and Gerri Knot vs. Northeast Southwest, et al.* illustrates some of the possibilities. In that fictional case, the board arranged meetings with candidate George Knot's wife and made the usual representation that the college had no substantial expectations of the candidate's spouse. A further statement concerning the activities of the previous spouse did not fairly reveal the board's or the

---

[61] A candidate's spouse in a recent search met a group of students with a hearty shout of "Let's get ready to party." This was not wise.

[62] Such as "He's a Muslim" or "She's not really American."

college's real expectations. On the one hand the board advised that there were no expectations, while secretly anticipating that Gerri Knot would perform the same services for the college that the outgoing president's spouse, Tina Tradition, had. When Gerri took the board at its word and disclosed her unavailability as the college's social hostess, George was cut from the candidate pool.

Discrimination between candidates on the basis of their marital status is illegal in at least twenty (20) states.[63] Under federal and state constitutions, states are prohibited from denying persons due process of law or the equal protection of the laws.[64] Although federal due process and equal protection guarantees have not yet been extended to discrimination based on marital status, state constitutions have been interpreted to permit the prohibition of such discrimination. The disqualification of George because his wife could not perform hostess and development work caused him to be treated differently than a candidate whose wife had a more flexible life (or was willing to pretend she did). This constitutes an unlawful discrimination.

There is the further problem of fraudulent advertising which arose because Northeast Southwest's ad made no reference to the need of a candidate to have a two-for-one spouse. The undisclosed requirement of a willing spouse was the requirement for want of which George lost his opportunity to be the President of Northeast Southwest and further lost his job at the

---

[63] www.unmarriedamerica.org.

[64] U.S. Constitution, amend. 14.

University of Contemplation. This forms a further basis for George's suit. The fact pattern of the *Knot vs. Northeast Southwest* case makes those plaintiffs' row tougher to hoe than would a fact pattern in which a candidate was single or gay. Likewise, plaintiff's case would be easier to make if the candidate's spouse suffered a legally recognized disability. In either of the former cases, the hiring of a married candidate with hosannas for the "little woman" who is going to help "move the college forward" gives the single or gay rejected candidate a prima facie case of marital and/or status discrimination. In the case of a spouse with a disability, the Americans with Disabilities Act would prohibit her being cut from the job of presidential spouse because of her apparent inability to serve as hostess conjoined with the failure of the college to give her a chance to request accommodations. In any of these cases, the college would have a significant uphill legal battle and considerable legal expenses to pay (even if it prevails in the litigation). Although most search committee and board meetings dealing with presidential candidate selection are supposed to be confidential, it is more often the case that they are not. The leaking of candidate identities, for example, is almost routine. Thus, if committee discussions are permitted to wander to the issue of the spouse, there is at least some likelihood that the committee's consideration of an unlawful criterion will be leaked. If this information gets out and there is a disgruntled candidate in receipt of the leak, a *Knot*-style complaint may be on the way.

Since the majority of college and university presidents are male, concerns about the wife are more common and relate to the interplay between the spouse on the one hand and the college and community constituencies on the other. The board really wants to know if the candidate's wife is crazy, unattractive, inarticulate, unpleasant, or (like Gerri Knot) largely unavailable. If she is absent, board or search committee members will want to know who is going to entertain potential donors at the president's house and represent the college in the local United Way drive. The law forbids the hiring institution to consider the hire to be a two-for-one transaction, but colleges have for so long considered the transaction to be just that, that it is hard to get them to consider the potential legal implications of issuing invitations to social occasions and house tours as a part of the search process.

Interestingly, the need to know about male spouses generally derives more from the relationship between the spouses themselves than from the potential relationship between the male spouse and the college community. What the male spouse will do in terms of relationship with faculty wives or United Way drives is generally of no particular moment (save to hope that his relationships with the former will be more formal and proper than those he may have with the latter). In the event of an absent male spouse, the greater board concern is often whether the female president will stay at the college, attending to college business, or whether she will feel the need to be off taking care of the husband at his location. This view denigrates both the president's sense of duty and the spouse's ability to tie his own shoelaces or find the refrigerator.

Because the focus of the board's concern is different with male spouses, a crazy, unattractive, inarticulate, or unpleasant male spouse is more likely to pass muster than his female counterpart. Apparently *he* can be ignored (or isolated) more deftly than *she* can. Because the drawing of such gender distinctions is probably unlawful, boards might better model their behaviors after the male spouse circumstance than the traditional behaviors demonstrated toward a female spouse.

"But wait, there's more!" The tradition of trustees or search consultants' telling candidates' spouses that nothing ("well, almost nothing") will be expected of them is not a helpful tradition, as the complaint of Cube Root illustrates. Here, the wife of the successful candidate found out too late that the demands of the college on her time and on the well-being of her family were a great deal more than she was initially told. Although the facts are somewhat hyperbolic, less extraordinary events have given rise to more dramatic legal complaints and some significantly large jury verdicts.

Most Americans are not expected to perform work without compensation. It is one thing to be a volunteer and quite another to be "volunteered."[65] Insofar as I have been able to determine, no presidential spouse has yet sued for the value of her contributions to a college or university. However, life being what it is in the twenty-first century, a suit to recover for this kind of value cannot be far off.

In addition to Fair Labor Standards Act and minimum-wage damages, other damages in such a case

---

[65] J. E. Clodius and D. S. Magrath, eds., *The President's Spouse: Volunteer or Volunteered* (Washington, D.C.: National Association of State Universities and Land-Grant Colleges, 1984).

could include the apparently remote damages which Cube Root alleges in her complaint (emotional distress and the consequential impacts on the children, etc.). Further, if Cube can make out a case of fraud or deceit or even reckless misrepresentation on the part of the board or any apparent agent of the board, punitive and exemplary damages and attorney's fees become clearly visible on the legal horizon. Such a claim would be grounded in the board's telling her that there were no significant expectations of her when it was common knowledge that the president's spouse had, historically, been expected to take on major responsibilities in the areas of hospitality and development.

The college could be expected to respond with the argument that Cube was acting as a volunteer, as had all of her predecessor presidential spouses, and thus had no expectation of compensation. As Hillary Clinton observed, "It's a role, not a job." The weakest part of this argument is the existence of compensated presidential spouses at other institutions of higher learning. The fact that other colleges are paying their presidents' spouses constitutes a recognition in the higher education business that the labor of the president's spouse has value worth paying for. Even if the college ultimately prevailed against Cube in court, the public relations implications of such a suit would be significantly damaging to the institution.[66]

---

[66] Again, I stress that no case has come to my attention in which claims such as these have been either alleged or proved. However, "novel" legal theories make for difficult cases on all sides.

Parents, teachers, and mentors teach that we should not expect something for nothing. That is a good lesson to take back to the search committee and the board of trustees. Hire a president and give him/her the resources needed to succeed. Leave the president's spouse out of it—or else.

CHAPTER 7

DOES SHE? OR DOESN'T SHE? ONLY THE DEVELOPMENT OFFICE KNOWS FOR SURE

Why does the college want or need the services of the president's spouse? Does the modern academy rely on the free or underpaid services of faculty spouses? Or deans' spouses? Or auxiliary-services spouses? Although Ms. President may once have been a quasi adoptive mother to the undergraduates, she rarely fulfills that role today. Depending on the finances and inertia of the particular college, the spouse may serve as custodian for the president's house, but usually this work is partially, if not substantially, done by regular college employees. For reasons of privacy, the president's house is usually divided into public and private space. The responsibility of the spouse, if any, should be for the private space only.

The service which colleges most frequently cite as justification for the employment (and in some cases enslavement) of the presidential spouse is development. The elements of that service vary by institution. In most instances, the female spouse is expected to create a warm and impressive home ethos and to maintain it in such a way that potential donors can be entertained at the president's house in a manner which will please and soothe them without instigating some prejudice which would impair that donor's instinct for giving. The décor must be grand enough to proclaim power and grace without offending the sensibilities of those donors who live more simply (or competing with those who live more lavishly).

The spouse is supposed to serve food and drink which will please without encouraging drunkenness, gluttony, or any other form of excess. All this must be done to widely different development targets. Surely, one cannot serve the board in the same manner as faculty, or staff, or local dignitaries, or, God forbid, students. "Important and generous" donors must be catered to in an altogether different manner. The risks of entertaining on the high end of this social spectrum are legion. The multi-course, multi-wine dinner which American University's president's spouse served to important people found itself set out in excruciating detail in the *Washington Post*. This level of entertaining constituted a major "oops" which contributed mightily to this president's early departure from the American University presidency.

The spouse must also serve as a form of accessory to the personage of the president. If the spouse is a woman, she must be forthright (but understated) and entertaining (but not too loud). If the spouse is a man, he must be deferential to the president and those members of the academy who are his betters. A friend of mine once described the role of the male presidential spouse thus: "Have you worked up your act of walking two paces behind the president with your hands clasped behind your back, while muttering something about 'saving the white rhino'?"

The female spouse must demonstrate a keen interest in football while betraying a girlish lack of knowledge of the game. The male spouse must know and love football without demonstrating an embarrassing under-knowledge of the game. These roles must be played out in all other athletic venues. There are numerous gender- and situation-specific behaviors which are expected of presidential spouses at concerts, galleries, lectures, and other grand occasions (commencement being the most obvious).

All of this posing has been and is being done in service to development. The important question is, "Does it really have any effect?" Statistical analysis of voluminous data could and probably should be undertaken on this question. However, a thorough gathering, crunching, and analysis of such data are beyond the scope of this work.

Nonetheless, a quick look at some of the data raises interesting questions for further study. The Council for Aid to Education of the RAND Corporation publishes an annual report on the fruits of development work done at most of the colleges and universities in America. The report is titled, for example, *2001 Voluntary Support of Education*.[67] For purposes of this chapter, I studied data from eleven colleges and universities.[68] The common factor among these colleges and universities was a

---

[67] Used by permission of Council for Aid to Education (CAE).

[68] Although eleven institutions were "assumption qualified," three reported data in such incomplete and inconsistent manners that they could not fairly be included in the review. Nonetheless, the development trends at these three colleges were consistent with trends at the remaining eight colleges.

transition from a male president to a female president. I assumed that the male presidents had more traditionally involved spouses and the female presidents had less-involved spouses.

This assumption was grounded in my experiences at AASCU and CIC conferences. For several years, both organizations have made a more concerted effort to include male spouses in spouse programs. Male spouses have been encouraged to participate both in mixed-gender spouse programs and in male-only programs. These programs have brought me into contact with a fairly representative sample of male presidential spouses. With the exception of the "new male spouses," which I will discuss in Chapter 9, the overwhelming majority of male spouses were not actively or prominently involved in development work.

I compared the development results reported by each of these schools for the three years before the male-to-female presidential transition and the three years after that transition.[69] If development was the primary justification for the spouse's contributory activities and if the male presidential spouses were less involved, would there be a falling off of the development performance following the transition from traditional female spouses to the less-involved male spouses?

The schools studied included large private, research/doctoral universities and smaller private master's/liberal arts colleges. All institutions studied were located east of the Mississippi, but were located from the Far North to the Deep South.

---

[69] In two of the eight schools, the transition allowed only two years of comparison on either side of the inauguration date.

The first comparison was based on what the Council for Aid to Education calls "Total Support."[70] The percent increase or decrease in receipt of Total Support for each institution for each year before and after its presidential transition was determined. These percentages were then aggregated for all pre- and post-transition years for all of the institutions combined. The outcomes were surprising. The average annual increase in the collection of Total Support for the pre-transition years was a little under 8 percent. The average annual increase in the collection of Total Support for the post-transition years was a little over 14 percent.

A further comparison was made of the statistics under the heading "Alumni Giving." The Council's reports allow a comparison of Alumni of Record with Alumni Donors. This comparison indicates what proportion of known graduates are actually giving. Again, the percentage of alumni donors (compared with the total number of known alumni) was determined for the three (or two) years before and after the presidential transition. All of these percentages were aggregated for the pre- and post-transition years. The aggregate rate of alumni contribution for the pre-transition years was almost 34 percent. The aggregate rate of alumni contribution for the post-transition years was almost 31 percent.

Other trends appeared in the data. A few of the pre-transition Total Support figures were dramatically higher in the transition year than the immediately

[70] "Total Support . . . reflects the total of both Outright Giving and Deferred Giving (FV). The sum of the columns under Outright Support for Current Operations, Outright Support for Capital Purposes and Deferred Giving . . . should be very close to the amount reported in Column 1 (Total Support)." Council for Aid to Education, *Voluntary Support of Education*, 2001.

preceding and immediately succeeding years. This seemed to suggest the conclusion of a capital campaign, after which the president retired. Also, where the Total Support had been regularly rising during the pre-transition years, the transition seemed to result in a slight dip in Total Support, followed by a rebound and a continuation of the upward trend which existed before the transition.

The number of factors which could bear on these statistics and perceived trends is infinite. Thus, it would be reckless to conclude that any particular president's spouse had anything to do with the increase or decrease of either Total Support or proportions of alumni participation. Although most of the transitions studied occurred in the 1990s, some went back to the late 1980s, and others occurred in this century. Factors such as the recession of the early 1990s, the market boom of the late 1990s, and the recession and jobless recovery of recent years could well affect the numbers, as well as the relative generosity of donors, alumni and non-alumni alike. Major institutional policy changes such as the termination of a long-standing program or the performance of an athletic team could affect development productivity. For example, one institution which was to be included in the study merged with another college. The commingling of donors to the one college which had a male president (and female spouse) with donors to the other college which had a female president (and a male spouse) made it impossible to make meaningful comparisons with the other colleges which were studied. In other instances the data provided in the Council's publication was extremely suspect. In one case, Alumni of Record for one year was reported as

27,000+ while in the next year it was reported as 11,000–. Either the numbers were wrong or one would not wish to be an alumnus/a of that college.[71]

However, with but one exception, the level of Total Support at each selected institution was higher two or three years after transition than it had been during the pre-transition years. Although the absolute causes of this phenomenon are not known, none of the data studied suggested that a diminution in development performance occurred after the appointment of women presidents. This was true of institutions both individually and collectively.

And so the question repeats: Do the good works of the traditional president's spouse have any effect on development? Although I cannot firmly conclude that they do not, the data suggest that not much is lost when the traditional arrangement (male president with female development helpmate) gives way to an arrangement in which the president's spouse is neither indentured to nor endangered by her role in the college. In fact, the numbers seem to indicate that the heavy lifting in development is done by the professionals the college hires and pays to do that lifting. These professionals are sometimes aided and abetted by the president's spouse. However, in other instances, the development personnel roll eyes and sigh at the approach of "that woman" or "that man." In general, development professionals seem to get along just fine without the assistance of the president's spouse and to complete their missions on their own. Some of the most effective and successful

---

[71] There was no practical way to determine if this disparity resulted from a clerical error by the compiler or an erroneous report by the college.

development officers work for colleges and universities headed by unmarried presidents.

Although my experience may be at odds with that of other presidential spouses, and notwithstanding many pleasant and thoughtful conversations I have had with major donors over the last twenty years, never once has a donor slapped down a multimillion-dollar check and declared, "Gosh darn it, if it hadn't been for that Dave fella, I would never have given this gift. How much more do you need?" If this has happened to other spouses, I suggest that the number of such happenings is really, really small, and that the emotional and personal prices which presidential spouses pay for this opportunity far exceeds the benefits which may flow to any particular college as the result of those spouses' efforts and sacrifices.

The deleterious effects of permitting (or requiring) a spouse to act in the role of the traditional presidential spouse, as described above, are numerous and serious. First and foremost is the resentment which builds up in most involved/traditional spouses over time. This resentment is generally more restrained for the unpaid spouse and generally more intense for the paid spouse. This resentment inevitably migrates to the president who is then put in the position of mediating between his spouse and the academic community for his spouse's salary, her title, and the various emoluments of her position.

The president is further exposed to a great range of adverse publicity and criticism arising from any expenditure which can be related to the spouse (this is doubly poisonous in difficult financial times). The ethical and legal issues raised by the two-for-the-price-of-one model are all the more troubling in a community which prides itself on rigorous and honest self-evaluation. So too is the unquestioned assumption that the actively involved spouse enhances development when the best she can do is maintain a neutral relationship with development professionals at the college while the worst she can do is extremely destructive of the esprit de corps of those professionals. These downside risks more than overbear the possible benefits.

CHAPTER 8
THE CONTRACT . . . YOU DO FOR ME—I DO FOR YOU

The history of presidential spousehood has largely been a history of women.[72] Women have traditionally served as social hostesses, development warriors, harried primary parents, gardeners, maintenance workers, and guardians of the etiquette of the campus. They continue to serve in some or all of these (and other) functions today.

Female college presidents are relatively new phenomena as are their male presidential spouses. As a general rule, the male spouses do not serve in the numerous roles in which their female counterparts have served. For whatever reasons, most male spouses have continued in their careers. Many have remained in the communities in which they lived before their spouses assumed the mantle of a college presidency. These male presidential spouses seem a happier lot than their sisters in presidential spousehood and are much less likely to proclaim that they "gave it all up to help/support the president."

There are, of course, notable exceptions to this rule. However, these exceptions seem to prove the rule that

---

[72] K. Koehler, ed., *The Evolving Role of the President's Spouse at the University of Michigan,* Michigan Historical Collections Bulletin, no. 37 (Ann Arbor, Mich.: Michigan Historical Collections, Bentley Historical Library, University of Michigan, 1989).

"giving it all up for the president" is not a good idea. The most wretched male presidential spouses of my acquaintance are those who left a job or community to accompany the new president and found themselves in places where their talents were unused and their minds were unengaged. They seemed to understand that it was not appropriate for them to participate in the day-to-day workings of the college, but found no activity that could substitute for their previous work life. In this circumstance, the male spouse has much in common with the female spouse who finds that the institution does not appreciate her contributions. The female spouse feels scorned or underappreciated; the male spouse feels abandoned and/or lost. They are both wretched.

The male spouse of a newly appointed female president usually brings a different template to his and the college's circumstances than does the female spouse of the male president. The former has typically been involved in his own professional or retirement pursuits, and boards usually do not mind if he continues to do so—provided he does not distract the president from her duties. He is treated differently from the female spouse who has traditionally been considered the "nurturer"— first of her family and later of the college. There is no ethical basis for this distinction. In my experience, the happiest and most fulfilled presidential spouses of both genders are the ones who have a career which is completely independent of the college with which their spouses are affiliated. In general, male spouses have been given a lot more "slack" in this regard by boards of trustees than have female spouses. The threat of legal action aside, it is simply not right to expect significant, free services to be performed for the college by the female spouse while the male spouse is free to pursue almost any activity that does not land him in jail. The longer, the louder, and the more repetitively this injustice is proclaimed and decried, the sooner it will go away.

Perhaps the arrival of male presidential spouses on the higher-education scene is the best news female spouses have had after centuries of unpaid service to higher education. The male spouses are, indeed, new creatures in the land of higher education. They are the "little children" of the institution, but they may, without intent, genius, or planning, have established a model for the liberation of female presidential spouses. On the other hand, some male presidential spouses are falling (or in some instances, charging) into the old traps which have ensnared female presidential spouses for generations. This development will be explored in Chapter 10.

If it has not become obvious in the foregoing, my professional training was that of a lawyer. I have long since concluded that the business of law schools is to take otherwise normally functioning brains and to twist them into what Harry Truman called "law brains." Law brains can fit any human experience into some niche or category which has been labeled and defined by some other law brains. Often, the fit of the human experience to the niche or category is clear only to other law brains. It is thus with some temerity that I apply the following quasi-legal analysis to the human experience of presidential spousehood.

Most lay thinking on the nature of the relationship between a presidential spouse and the college begins with the notion that there is some duty on the part of the spouse to the college. The spouse is thereby inclined to think that there is, or should be, a reciprocal duty of the college to her. It is a short step from this kind of thinking to a sense or feeling on the part of one of these parties or the other that some kind of contractual relationship has arisen between them. If there is a contract, what kind of contract is it? Into which niche or category does it fit?

A contract is an agreement which the law will enforce between the parties to that agreement. A contract may arise from the express promises of the parties (an express contract) or may arise from the conduct of the parties even though there are no expressed promises. The latter type of contract is known as an "implied" contract. Contracts may also be enforced to prevent one party from unfairly taking advantage of another party, notwithstanding that there has been no express agreement and no conduct from which a court might find an "implied" contract. Such contracts are called "quasi contracts." It is important to note that "quasi" and "implied" contracts only arise when the fact pattern of the particular case is similar to ones in which courts have previously determined that a "quasi" or "implied" contract exists. There is little judicial inclination to find a quasi or implied contract without a precedent.

In a very few instances, express contracts exist between the spouses of presidents and the colleges which they serve. More often, a spouse believes that by reason of her work and the college's expectations, a contract may, or should, be "implied." The vast majority of president's spouses with whom I have come into contact believe that absent an express or implied contract, there should be a "quasi" contract in order to prevent the college from taking advantage of them. Any review of the literature in this area reveals the frequency with which the concept of the president's spouse having a job is repeated. Surely, a job cannot exist in the absence of a contract—be that contract express, implied, or quasi. It is a short step from the notion that the president's spouse has a job/contract with the college to the serious legal and organizational consequences which I have previously discussed. Whether it be for good or ill, I have found no case in which a court has found that an implied or quasi contract existed between a spouse and a college, save one domestic relations case in which a spouse was awarded temporary use of the president's house during the pendency of a divorce.

Commentators continue to assert that it is the responsibility of boards and search committees to clearly articulate what the institution expects of Mr. or Ms. Incoming Spouse. This misses the point. Absent an express contract between the spouse and the board (the wisdom of which is questioned above), there is no contract between the incoming spouse and the board.[73] There is no contract between the spouse and the college. There is a contract between the president-elect and the board. If boards and search committees need education, it is to the notion that having expectations of the spouse is very dangerous, both for the institution and for the spouse. If the board demands work for which it does not

---

[73] Except in those instances where the board makes a contract with the incoming spouse to do a job for which there was no competition, i.e. being the president's spouse. Except for a few rural locations in the Southwest, only one person at a time can possibly qualify for this job.

intend to pay, fair labor standards or minimum wage considerations may be implicated. Even if the spouse is willing to do the work to fulfill the expectations of the board and/or the traditions of her predecessors, the inevitable conflicts between the spouse and other institutional employees will be damaging to the spouse's sense of belonging and to her loyalty to the college and possibly to her loyalty to the president.

There is a further reason why contractual relations between the board and the president's spouse are inherently suspect. It is fundamentally unfair to expect a spouse who is usually very supportive of the presidential candidate to negotiate forcefully with the very persons who have the power to dump her husband/candidate out of the search. The temptation to be accommodating is almost irresistible. When my wife was interviewed for the two presidencies in which she ultimately served, neither the board nor the search committee mentioned any institutional expectation for me. Nonetheless, I specifically raised the topic. I did so with considerable trepidation, because I well knew that my statement could imperil my wife's chances.

I could only rationalize my forthrightness (or, perhaps better, foolhardiness) by believing that the college would be happier to find out about my unavailability before selecting my wife than after. In both instances the boards indicated that there were no expectations for my availability. To their credits, they meant what they said. To the extent that I have performed services which were helpful to the colleges at which my wife has served as president (and there were many), those services were performed in connection with understandings *between my wife and me.*

For boards, there is a flip side to the problem of spouse contracts. As a result of my participation in presidential searches in which my wife was a candidate and, further, of conversations I have had with other candidates' spouses over the last twenty-plus years, I know that because of the power imbalance between the board and the potential presidential spouse, the spouse is unlikely to raise the question of the college's expectations until after the board has selected the president. From the board's point of view, should the spouse raise questions about her role after her husband is selected, she will appear to be making demands which should have been raised in the original discussions with the candidate. In some of these instances, the board feels that it is being bushwhacked. This does not create an environment which is healthy for either the board or the spouse. The imbalance of powers between the board and the spouse and the impossibility of good timing of the spouse's expressions of concern make this phase of the presidential search very tricky.

If there is any appropriate contract among the president, the spouse, and the college, it is more in the nature of what the law brains call a "third-party beneficiary contract." In such a contract, A agrees with B to perform some act for the benefit of C. The most familiar third-party beneficiary contract is probably a motor vehicle liability insurance policy in which the driver (A) and the insurance company (B) agree that should the driver injure a third party (C), the insurance company will pay for the damages. In the college presidency context it is arguable that in addition to the express contract between A, the president, and C, the board, there is an additional third-party contract among

A, the president, B, the spouse, and C, the college. In this context, the president and the spouse should decide upon what, if any, service spouse B will perform for the college. If B is to be compensated, it is to A (the president) that she should look. This arrangement keeps C (the college) out of any legal or ethical relationship with the spouse, thus insulating it and her from most of the problems which have been discussed earlier.

As a general rule of law, third-party beneficiary contracts may not be enforced against the insurer by the beneficiary. Thus a person injured by a negligent driver cannot sue the driver's insurance company. He can only sue the negligent driver. This is particularly apt for the college president's spouse: the college cannot enforce the contract against the spouse because it has no contract with her—only with the president.

In the traditional presidential spouse model, a contract is made between A (the president) and C (the college) to the detriment of B (the spouse). The spouse (who has no status or leverage) is burdened with duties which she performs as a sort of dowry to the college. Since the college was kind enough to hire her husband, she will perform uncompensated and underappreciated work during the entirety of the president's tenure. Thus, the party with the least bargaining power (the spouse) has the regimen of her life established by others. This sounds more than a bit quaint and outdated.

Although I have suggested that the spouse's duties should be limited to those upon which the president and the spouse agree, I can envision a situation in which such negotiations lead to the spouse's life looking just like traditional college presidents' spouses lives have looked for centuries. The objective of the negotiations should not be to replicate the pitfalls and miseries of the past, but to provide the college with just enough spouse presence, combined with the assignment of most spouse duties to regular college employees, to allow it to break the habit of needing the spouse.

Are there no happy presidential spouses? Of course there are, and they pursue their lives in a tremendous variety of styles. I repeat here for emphasis that there are presidential spouses who serve their spouses' colleges in very traditional ways and who are as delighted with their situations as the colleges who benefit from their good works are delighted to have them. For them this work has little to offer other than to suggest that their successors may not fare as well as they have—that a pattern is being established or continued which will bring more successors to woe than to delight.

Often, boards and college communities have expectations of performance by presidential spouses which arose from the relationship which the board and community had with the outgoing presidential spouse. If Mrs. Outgoing Spouse entertained the faculty wives in the garden on Tuesday afternoons, Ms. Incoming Spouse had jolly well better do the same thing. Depending on the length of institutional memory, the traditions of several generations of presidential spouses can end up in the lap and on the calendar of Ms. Incoming. These traditions can be a cruel legacy for the new president's spouse.

For all of the other spouses who do feel resented, taken advantage of, and in a few cases even hated, there are alternatives. And most of the alternative styles of being a college president's spouse should be grounded in Polonius' admonition, "This above all, to thine own self be true."[74] Preliminarily, this principle seems simple enough. However, in the real world the principle can easily be lost by even the most stalwart practitioner of sensible presidential spousehood.

The difficulty arises from the college's innate tendency to flatter (at least initially) the president's spouse. This flattery proceeds from the assumption that if the president is smart and accomplished, the president's spouse must be smart and accomplished, too. Generally this is a correct assumption, but the spouse is rarely well served in acting upon it. Even if the spouse is smart and accomplished, that fact does not justify her assuming official or semiofficial duties, even if she is invited to do so. If my neighbor thinks I am a kind and generous person, I am flattered by that opinion. Nonetheless, that opinion does not give me the right to use his car or his lawn mower or to boss his kids around. If I do (even at his suggestion) use the car or the lawn mower or boss his kids, our relationship will suffer.

What is very rarely said at spouse seminars is the simple statement that, in a considerable majority of situations, it is *fun* to be the spouse of a college president. The academy is a fascinating, contentious, lively, and nurturing place. The energy generated by college students can be experienced viscerally. Hang around a predominantly undergraduate campus for a semester or two and then remain on the campus through graduation. The whole feeling of the place changes as students decamp for the summer—the magic departs.

---

[74] Shakespeare, *Hamlet*, act 1, scene 3, line 78, in *The Complete Works of William Shakespeare*, ed. W. A. Wright (Garden City, N.Y.: Doubleday, 1936).

The feeling changes again as the students return in the late summer and the energy level rises.

If being around a large body of young people whose mental and physical faculties are at the highest levels they will achieve in their lifetimes does not stir wonder and admiration, your senses are slipping. Could you take on a schedule of four or five undergraduate courses, participate in a sport, assume a student leadership role, and maintain a social life? If your capacity for this level of activity is somewhat lower than it was when you were an undergraduate, you can at least stand back and admire the young people who have that capacity now.

As the president's spouse, you don't have to be a player—it's OK to be a spectator. Appreciate the energy. Attend the concerts, lectures, and sporting events. Prowl the library. Seek out and appreciate those special places which exist on every campus where peace of mind and the joys of quiet contemplation can be found. Admire your spouse's ability to captain an apparently unmanageable ship. But always remember, you're the captain's spouse, not the First Mate (even it is your first marriage). Enjoy everything—just don't try to run the ship.

CHAPTER 9

"SHE'S JUST A VOLUNTEER . . . SO WHAT'S THE PROBLEM?"

While most objective observers would agree that having the president's spouse *employed* by the college could raise issues of nepotism, many board members, presidents, and spouses fail to anticipate the mischief which a spouse serving as a *volunteer* to the college could create. The thinking goes something like this: "Since we're not actually employing the spouse and the spouse will not have actual authority over college employees and she won't have an actual budget to spend, what harm can come of her acting as a volunteer, say in the development office?"

The board and the university community at the University of Vermont experienced the flaw in that line of thought. In the summer of 2002, the University of Vermont selected Daniel Mark Fogel as its president. Two of Fogel's recent predecessors had served short presidencies, leaving under difficult and contentious circumstances. The university was very invested in having a successful, relatively long-term president. Fogel had served in various faculty and administrative positions at Louisiana State University from 1976 to 2002. He was serving as provost at LSU when he was selected to lead UVM.

Fogel was accompanied to Vermont by his wife, Rachel Kahn-Fogel. Fogel and his wife had met in seventh grade, marrying while he was in graduate school in the 1970s. Kahn-Fogel was an artist, exhibiting several of her works at art shows at the University of Vermont. Serving as the president's spouse, Kahn-Fogel also volunteered in the university development office, planning events. The confluence of the president's spouse and event planning is fairly common in colleges and universities because the president's house is often the location of many development events.

Interestingly, the nexus of development and the president's house did not exist at the University of Vermont because Fogel had declined to live in the traditional president's house, citing general noise and partying in the immediate campus vicinity as a reason. Nonetheless, Kahn-Fogel continued to work in the development office, planning events far from the traditional sinecure of the president's spouse—the president's house.

President Fogel's tenure was generally considered successful. He developed a ten-year vision for the university, raised substantial sums of money, increased enrollment, and built several new facilities. In March 2011 Fogel announced his intended retirement in July 2012.

In May 2011, less than one week following the University of Vermont's graduation ceremonies, two Burlington newspapers, the *Burlington Free Press* and *Seven Days*, reported that Kahn-Fogel had been involved in what was reported as a "relationship" with one Michael Schultz, an associate vice president for development and alumni affairs.[75]

The relationship had been discovered by Schultz's wife, Pauline Manning, in early 2010, when she found letters from Kahn-Fogel addressed to her husband at a post office box unknown to her. The letters were lengthy and vivid with descriptions of romantic behaviors which could be interpreted as real or as fantasies. Whatever explanations Schultz had, Manning was not convinced. She filed for divorce. The case came on for trial in February 2011. A portion of the trial transcript was reproduced in *Seven Days*, which showed the trial judge trying mightily to keep one of the letters out of the admitted exhibits in the case.[76] Although the letters were not admitted into evidence, the transcript included enough detail to fire up investigative reporters at both the *Free Press* and *Seven Days*.

The headlines read,

"At UVM, personal crisis becomes public concern"[77]

and

"Dangerous Liaisons: Fair Game: A relationship between the wife of UVM president Dan Fogel and a

---

[75] S. Hemingway, "At UVM, personal crisis becomes public concern," *Burlington Free Press*, May 25, 2011, p. A1; S. Totten, "Dangerous Liaisons," *Seven Days*, May 25, 2011, pp. 12–15.

[76] "[Judge] Katz: It strikes me that we had a little discussion in chambers earlier. Having this letter in a public file does not enhance job security, when job security is in mutual interest. It's not just one side's interest." Totten, "Dangerous Liaisons," p. 14.

[77] Burlington Free Press May 25, 2011, p. A1.

top fundraiser is raising questions—and eyebrows— at the state university." [78]

By May 28, 2011, conservative blogger Robert Stacy McCain was writing about the Fogel-Kahn/Schultz affair, opining by some opaque logic that the Kahn/Fogel situation demonstrated a tendency on the part of academics with Ph.D.s to condescend to non-academics without Ph.Ds.[79]

Had Kahn-Fogel become involved with someone not a part of the UVM staff, the story would probably been over by May 29 (or sooner). Unfortunately, Schultz was an associate vice president in the very department in which Kahn-Fogel volunteered. She worked with him regularly, eventually involving him in the resolution of a dispute between between Fogel and Kahn-Fogel on the one hand and a different vice president for development on the other. Later, when the new vice president for development stopped assigning Schultz to work with Kahn-Fogel, she made repeated attempts to have him reassigned to work with her. Her requests were not granted.[80]

The soup became thicker still when it was discovered that Schultz had recently been awarded a

---

[78] Hemingway, "Personal crisis"; Totten, "Dangerous Liaisons."

[79] R. S. McCain, "Another Reminder That the Academic Elite Are Your Moral Superiors," May 28, 2011, http://theothermccain.com/2011/05/28/another-reminder-that-the-academic-elite-are-your-moral-superiors/ (accessed March 20, 2013).

[80] Totten, "Dangerous Liaisons."

UVM Ph.D. based in part on a dissertation he had written entitled "Elucidating the Role of the University CEO's Spouse in Development, Alumni Relations, and Fund Raising." This discovery called into question the process by which the Ph.D. had been granted and created another potential problem for the board to investigate.

Adding to the carnival atmosphere, Schultz was reported to have come out as a gay man following his wife's discovery of the Kahn-Fogel letters. Fogel completed the surreal tableau, announcing that "Rachel has asked me to let it be known that she has long been in treatment for serious mental health issues with which she has struggled throughout her life."[81]

The UVM board dutifully took on the tasks of reviewing and investigating the various problems raised by the disclosures. Among the issues raised were: sexual harassment, use of college funds, the awarding of Schultz's Ph.D., assignment practices in the development office, and college policies related to the role of the president's spouse/partner. Personnel both in and outside the UVM community were engaged in this effort.

The governor of Vermont is an ex officio member of the UVM board. Governor Peter Shumlin weighed in on the controversy, saying, "This is an unfortunate story— and a very personal one . . . And, as a UVM trustee, I support the actions of the Board of Trustees to conduct a comprehensive objective review of this situation to insure the University practices, policies and standards of conduct have been appropriately followed . . . I, like the

---

[81] Hemingway, "Personal crisis," p. A4.

rest of the trustees, will await the result of this review before making any further comment." [82]

On July 31, 2011, Fogel resigned effective immediately and was replaced on an interim basis by the provost. His previous announcement of a July 2012 retirement date contemplated his receiving his $410,000-per-year salary for one year. He would then return to the English faculty at an annual salary of $195,000. This retirement package raised little comment at the time of Fogel's initial retirement announcement—notwithstanding the fact that his faculty salary would surpass the salary of the most senior English Department faculty by $80,000.

The initially restrained reaction to the financial aspects of Fogel's departure gave way to unrestrained indignation by August 11, 2011, when the *Burlington Free Press* headline trumpeted,

"PAYDAY AT UVM."[83]

In an apparent attempt to entice Fogel into leaving the presidency posthaste, an additional five (5) months of presidential salary was offered—and accepted. The *Burlington Free Press*'s greater indignation was lavished on Michael Schultz, whose severance package was fully described in a lower headline. He was offered seventeen months of salary (approximately $220,000), health benefits through 2012, and $15,000 in attorney's

---

[82] Ibid., p. A1.

[83] T. Johnson, "Payday at UVM," *Burlington Free Press*, August 11, 2011, p. A1.

fees, which he accepted. All of these board actions were taken following a determination that "No laws or policies were violated . . . but employee morale suffered under *the ambiguous authority exercised by the university president's wife* (emphasis added). The institution must now clarify the role of the presidential spouse and formally review its commitment to a decent workplace climate."[84]

The board's reference to "a decent workplace climate" together with the size of the Schultz settlement strongly suggested that the so-called "relationship" between Kahn-Fogel and Schultz was largely a product of Kahn-Fogel's imagination. Nonetheless, Schultz was now damaged goods. He could not be retained in the development office and had to be bought out. The board likely had enjoyed a positive relationship with Kahn-Fogel and her husband and did not want to further embarrass either of them with a public airing of its detailed findings. The board would receive substantial public recrimination for this decision.

Leading the recrimination was a member of the board, Governor Peter Shumlin. Shumlin had not participated in the board's investigation or discussion of the Kahn-Fogel/Schultz matter, stating, "I've got my hands full running the State of Vermont."[85] Following the board's decisions, however, in a conversation which Fogel believed was private, Shumlin urged him to decline his severance package, creating a scholarship

---

[84] Ibid., p. A1

[85] T. Hallenbeck, "Shumlin's Saturday Phone Call," *Burlington Free Press*, August 12, 2011, p. A4.

with the proceeds. Fogel declined. A few days thereafter the Burlington Free Press headlines proclaimed,

"SHUMLIN'S SATURDAY PHONE CALL—

Governor suggests Fogel start scholarship with compensation package"

and

"I thought my conversation with the governor was private, I was disappointed he made it public— Former University of Vermont President Daniel Fogel."[86]

Neither man emerged from this exchange looking the better for the experience. Fogel looked greedy and Shumlin had seriously "dissed" the board of directors of which he was a member, for a decision in which he had chosen not to participate.

The University of Vermont has adopted a new policy. A copy of that policy is set out in Appendix D. It prohibits the president's spouse/partner from supervising university staff and spending university money. It does not address the problem of long-term volunteering by a president's spouse/partner. Interestingly, the Kahn-Fogel situation involved neither staff supervision nor the expenditure of university funds. The policy wisely anticipates some problems without clearly addressing the phenomenon which contributed

---

[86] Ibid., p. A1.

154

greatly to the university's May-to-August 2011 distress.[87]

Presidential spouse/partner volunteering has a long history in American higher education. No doubt, some colleges and universities benefit from the services spouse/partners provide. However, this kind of arrangement does create risks for the institution, its board, its staff, its finances, its students, and its relationship with the larger community. Boards should institute policies and practices which welcome the president's spouse/partner to the university community and which encourage her to participate in the life of the learning community. These policies should also inform the spouse/partner that her life should be focused on the larger community and that *long-term* volunteering will not be a part of her role. Finally, these policies and practices should inform the spouse/partner that her defining relationship will be with her spouse/partner president, not with the university.[88]

---

[87] The policy is not without its detractors. A participant at a recent ACE conference described the new UVM policy as "punishment" of the new presidential spouse for the bad behavior of her predecessor. I disagree, considering the new policy as guidance, not punishment.

[88] When the president's spouse/partner (and family) reside in a President's House, scheduling of events at that house needs to be made with the spouse/partner. The spouse/partner should not have substantial involvement in planning and execution of such events beyond issues of schedule. Her opinions on planning and execution (should she have them) should be expressed to and through the president.

CHAPTER 10

WHERE THE BOYS ARE

Male spouse attendance at presidential spouse programs has undergone a significant change in recent years. Back in the late 1980s our numbers were tiny, but in very recent years the numbers have been going up, appreciably. At one conference session I attended in early 2006, 20 percent of the attendees were men.

In the past, men were extremely unlikely to participate actively in these programs. By this I mean that the men rarely spoke. When they did speak, they usually distinguished their experiences from those of the female spouses and that was it. Little was expected of them by their wives' board members or the board members' spouses. They were pretty much free to hunt and/or gather as their instincts and preferences dictated.

I do not have a sense that college/university board members' attitudes toward male spouses have changed much. However, some male spouses' perceptions of the significance and importance of their roles/jobs at their respective colleges have changed—radically. Members of this minority male spouse community envision themselves somewhat as female spouses have envisioned themselves for many decades. They consider themselves to be jobholders with significant responsibilities to the college community. And they believe the college community, reciprocally, has responsibilities to them. Boards should keep a particularly wary eye on what I call the "new male spouses."

As a group, male spouses tend to be older than their spouse/presidents. They are more likely to be either employed or retired. Rarely have they given up a career to help the president. And the new male spouses are very self-assured and self-confident. Unlike most of the female spouses, these new male spouses seem emotionally immune to the criticisms which so often wound female spouses. Where a female spouse might feel disrespected by a "who the hell do you think you are" comment, the new male spouse would more likely respond, "I'm the president's husband—that's who. Do you want to make something of it?" The wellsprings of spouses' perceptions of their roles are the same for most female and new male spouses, but these new guys are bulked up on metaphorical steroids.

Example 1: I observed a third-year male presidential spouse who had been living in the president's house during renovations. He stated that the house had not been occupied by the previous president and that it needed a great deal of work. As the work progressed, this spouse took on the role of a supervisor of the project. There was no suggestion that the college had asked him to do so or that he had sought the input of others, he just believed it was his personal prerogative.

He described his observations of the men working on the project and the reasons which caused him to conclude that these men were not putting in a day's work for a day's pay. He was quite proud that his complaints caused most of the workers to be fired. He was even prouder of his actions relating to the buildings and grounds supervisor. This president's spouse was sufficiently disagreeable in that relationship that the supervisor quit. The president's spouse claimed these actions were enthusiastically received by the college community because they had saved the college a lot of money and because no one really liked the now-departed supervisor.

However, a few sentences later he declared that he was "always a target." Although he did not identify the people who were aiming at him, there were clearly several of them out there. He believed that if "they" couldn't "get the president," "they" would "take shots" at him. He seemed to genuinely enjoy this situation, stating, "I like to be part of the action."

I wonder if this is the environment which the board anticipated when it appointed this man's wife to be the president. Certainly, if someone is stealing the college silverware, a call to campus security would be in order, but there is a limit on how intrusive a spouse can be before institutional resentment and the consequences of the same begin to pile up.

This spouse further claimed that certain members of the college community were so delighted with the departure of the buildings and grounds supervisor that they gave him "cases of tequila." Thus his attitudes and activities appeared to have created a serious conflict not only between the spouse and some of the regular college employees (those who were shooting at him) but also between different groups of college employees (pro-supervisor and anti-supervisor).

His activities suggest that he thinks he knows much more about personnel matters than the administrators who were hired to supervise college employees—the administrators who report to his wife. If he is right on that point, I would suggest that anything beyond a "gee, honey, there seems to be a problem with . . ." should be flagged for Excessive Spousal Interference. If, after the "gee, honey . . ." hint has been given, nothing changes, it is probably time to either get out of Dodge or shut up.

Although some spouses have constitutions which permit them to tough out controversies such as these, usually the collective strength of the institution is greater than that of the spouse, causing the latter (and his spouse) to give way or give up. Even if so dire a consequence does not befall this president and her spouse, the cooperative fabric of the college has been unnecessarily damaged by his intrusive behaviors.

Example 2: In this instance, a first-year presidential spouse asserted even greater authority at what he referred to as "his college."[89] He stated that the college had hired both his wife and him as a "team"; that the college knew that he would have powers equivalent to those of his wife; that the board was seeking just this kind of a partners arrangement when it hired "them"; that the board wanted him to play "a significant role" at the college; that his authority in all matters was "implied"; and that he superintended college facility issues "directly." He went on to describe initiatives he

---

[89] Use of possessive language like this is not limited to higher education. Athletic teams which used to be referred to as "they" are now called "we." The Red Sox did not win yesterday; "we" did. Use of this kind of language has (properly) left some of its speakers quite embarrassed. "A new university president once made the mistake of referring to the people on the academic side of the university as 'my faculty,' and was immediately corrected. A professor said to him 'You may be our president, sir, but we are not your faculty.'" Muriel Beadle, *Where Has All the Ivy Gone?* (Garden City, N.Y.: Doubleday, 1972), pp. 160–161.

had undertaken to establish and coordinate an exchange program with a foreign government.

In all of these matters, he did not speak of consultative relationships with other members of the college community. There were simply areas in which he believed that he was knowledgeable and that he implicitly had the authority to act on the college's behalf. He repeatedly referred to himself and his wife as a "power couple" and seemed to consider the college very fortunate to have "their" services.

This spouse is still very new to his situation. It is impossible to determine, at this early stage, how the college will respond to his attitudes and behaviors. I have read many *Chronicle of Higher Education* presidential search announcements. Nowhere have I seen such an announcement mention the powers, actual or implied, of the anticipated president's spouse. Nowhere did such announcements suggest that the institution was seeking a "power couple."[90] Time will tell.[91]

As the numbers of male presidential spouses grow and as more of these new male spouses begin to participate in the institutional lives of the colleges their wives were tapped to lead, will the colleges come to view these men differently than they viewed the female presidential spouses who preceded them? In the past, boards considered that it was OK when male spouses

---

[90] Had it done so, it would have illegally discriminated against potential candidates who were unmarried.

[91] A few years into this presidency, the spouse appeared at another spouses' event. He seemed to be much less assertive about his prerogatives and perhaps a bit chastened. His wife's web page and biography make no mention of him. Perhaps time has told.

steered clear of the nuts-and-bolts operations of the college. This had not been the case for their female predecessors. What will colleges do with gentlemen like those described above, who forcefully grab the college bull by its institutional horns? These guys will not shrink under the withering glance of some trustee's wife or the bristling hostility of a superintendent of buildings and grounds.

The difference in attitudes/behaviors between the new male spouses and traditional female spouses was nicely illustrated in one of the spouse seminars I recently attended. Throughout the early days of the program various speakers made references to a topic which seemed to be of very broad and deep interest to most of the participants. That topic was aired on the last day of the program and the session was very well attended. There were fifty-one (80 percent) female spouses and thirteen (20 percent) male spouses present. Early in the session, the presenter entertained questions. Fully 75 percent of the time given over to questions was taken up by a very small group of male spouses—and most of that time was not spent on real questions as much as it was given over to "questions designed to *impart* rather than to *elicit* information."[92] These guys are coming down the pike right now and boards had best be prepared to deal with them.

In the current environment, I believe that a strong, assertive male presidential spouse can usually win board tolerance of his interference with the work of regular employees of the college. I believe that a strong,

---

[92] Ralph L. MacDonald, Jr., observation.

assertive female presidential spouse can occasionally win board tolerance of such interference. However, board tolerance should not be taken as the measure of the appropriateness of such spouse participation. The board only represents the college; it is not the college. The spousal rubber meets the institutional road when the spouse engages the sensibilities of regular college employees. These employees constitute a proud group with very old and much-honored traditions. Administrators come and go, but the college endures. It may suffer more or less silently, but in the end, it will be there educating students long after the president and her spouse have faded from memory. Given a test of wills between a president's spouse (male or female) and the academy, my money will always be on the academy. Spouses occasionally win a battle, but the college nearly always wins the war.

It is the board's responsibility to set conditions which will diminish the likelihood of either a battle or a war. These new male spouses are out there. They are coming to a campus near you. They portend significant difficulties for the college community. They are certainly less sympathetic figures than some of their female counterparts simply because of their Kevlar™ self-confidence.

The board's concerns should be twofold: The first issue is the ethical one. Notwithstanding the new male spouse's willingness to endure (and even revel in) the slings and arrows of outrageous collegiate fortune, is it ethical for the colleges to expect or accept his labors? The answer to that question, when it was raised concerning the labors of traditional female presidential spouses, was "no." I can see no ethical distinction which would cause the answer to become "yes" when it comes to male presidential spouses—even those who yearn for the rough and tumble of the big game.

The second issue is a practical one. Past and present experience teaches us that the exercise of assumed, implicit, or implied supervisory authority by a presidential spouse plows a fertile field for the sowing of institutional discontent. The quiet, friendly, and devilishly clever spouse may succeed in the discreet exercise of supervisory authority, but the louder, the more hostile, and the more blunt the exercise of such authority becomes, the greater institutional resentment will become and the greater will be the problem with which the board has to deal.

The addition of money to the mix will cause an exacerbation of the problems. I have no reason to believe that the new male spouses will be reluctant to demand compensation for their jobs. Because our society has a much greater tolerance for female volunteering and sacrifice than for male volunteering and sacrifice, I believe that predominantly male boards will be more receptive to the compensation demands of male spouses than they have been to the demands of female spouses. Should boards succumb to these demands, they will encounter the kind of discontent which arises when any presidential spouse receives pay for this noncompetitive position. In addition they will face the complaints of those who perceive unfairness in paying the male spouse when his female predecessor was uncompensated.

That very circumstance has arisen at the University of Iowa. Following the selection of a new president in 2007, negotiations began for Dr. Sally Mason's compensation package. Both the *Des Moines Register* and the *Iowa City Press Citizen* reported that the new president requested that her husband, Dr. Kenneth Mason, be employed half-time as a biology lecturer and half-time as a fund-raiser for UI. His total salary would exceed $100,000.

The interim president contacted the University of Iowa Foundation at the request of the UI board, asking the foundation to pay roughly half of the total Kenneth Mason package. The foundation agreed.

As reported in the *Des Moines Register*, Kenneth Mason is receiving about $107,000 per year, $54,175 of which is paid for fund-raising activities.[93] Of the approximately $107,000 total salary, $72,000 is reported to come from the University of Iowa Foundation.[94]

Casting a cloud over these arrangements is the apparent lack of documentation of Kenneth Mason's employment agreement[95] and differing recollections of its terms and circumstances by representatives of the university board, the foundation board, and the former interim president. Potential questions regarding how Kenneth Mason is being paid a full-time lecturer's salary plus a half-time fund-raiser's salary remain.

However, the most disturbing aspect of the arrangement is its uniqueness in Iowa public higher education. *Women in Higher Education* noted that *female* presidential spouses at Iowa's other public

---

[93] C. Kauffman, "Foundation Head: U of I Official Sought Pay for Ken Mason," *Des Moines Register*, May 25, 2012.

[94] C. Kauffman, "Ken Mason's Jobs Never Put on Paper," *Des Moines Register*, May 23, 2012.

[95] Ibid.

universities (Iowa State and Northern Iowa) are *not* paid for similar fund-raising activities.[96] No doubt there will be ongoing discussions about how male and female presidential spouses are/are not compensated in Iowa.

I have made several trips to remote areas of the eastern Canadian Arctic. This is referred to as being "out on the land." On each trip I have been told by the Royal Canadian Mounted Police (RCMP) to be wary of polar bears. The bears are strong, fast, and possessed of such a keen sense of smell that they can hunt prey from twenty miles away—and they do occasionally hunt humans. The RCMP also advised that mature bears are usually not a problem. It is the adolescent males who cause most of the fatal interactions. As the new male spouse enters upon his new life in the academy, he is a functional adolescent. Boards should beware.

Boards and search committees should inform new presidents that their spouses have not been hired; that there are no expectations for their spouses' services; and that spouses should not anticipate exercising any authority over employees of the college.[97] The more self-confident and assertive the new spouse is, the more emphatic should be the board's instruction.

---

[96] "Pay Presidential Spouse? Iowa Wonders," *Women in Higher Education* 21, no. 6 (June 2012): 4.

[97] I will admit an exception to this rule when the issue concerns the private areas of the President's house

CHAPTER 11

NOW THE TROUBLE WITH ALL THIS KNOWLEDGE I'VE GOT HOLD OF IS . . . THAT IT'S USELESS [98]

This was the lament of comedian Peter Cook as he portrayed a man who wanted to be a judge but ended up being a coal miner because he lacked a working knowledge of Latin. Although the man takes solace in "the world of lit'rature," he concludes that "all this knowledge I've got hold of . . . is useless."[99] A similar lament is expressed by many college presidential spouses. She's got hold of a lot of knowledge, but if she does not participate actively in the life of her campus, is it all useless? If she fades into an imitation of my minister's wife (Chapter 2 (C)), what good is she to the higher educational community? Is there a role for her?

I have yet to meet a presidential spouse who lacks an inquisitive nature and substantial intelligence. Being possessed of these attributes, each and every presidential spouse of my acquaintance has acquired a working knowledge of the overall affairs of colleges which is second to none. Through daily experience, reading of

---

[98] Peter Cook, *Beyond the Fringe*, Alexander H. Cohen Production, 1960.

[99] Ibid.

relevant books and periodicals, management of the presidential household, and the sharing of the hopes, aspirations, and fears of the president, the presidential spouse gets hold of a lot of knowledge. Among the skills acquired and lessons learned are:

--Keeping a schedule which integrates with the Alice-in-Wonderland schedule of the president teaches that even the energy of the most boundlessly energetic president has its limits;

--Keeping company with a "generous donor" whose manners and personal habits resonate most closely with those of an alpha wolf teaches restraint, diplomacy, and sophisticated self-defense;[100]

--Keeping track of the tortured, Byzantine maze of the college budget is not a required subject, but what presidential spouse has not endured late-night ruminations of the president as he mulls the factors and fancies which may or will cause the college budget to become unbalanced; this process teaches that (with diligent application and creativity) these problems usually work out;

--Keeping track of both the wisdom and the mean-spiritedness of government officials as they alternately promote and burden higher education teaches that there is no arena of human endeavor in which selflessness and extreme pandering to callow self-interest can so happily coexist as they can in a legislature;

--Keeping in mind the names and interests of all of those student leaders, faculty members, citizens,

---

[100] In fact the college presidential spouse is frequently "requested" to look after the most disagreeable guests at many college functions.

administrators, staff, plumbers, electricians, food service personnel, campus security officers, and the spouses, kids, and (sometimes) pets of all the foregoing teaches that Dale Carnegie and all of those other memory guys had some really good ideas;

--Keeping the moat full, the alligators hungry, and the drawbridge up when the forces of unreason seize significant numbers of students or faculty teaches self-preserving calm in the face of occasionally outrageous provocation;

--Keeping in mind that the best policy usually parallels lessons learned in kindergarten teaches both the president and the spouse that simple principles often govern apparently complex situations;

--Keeping in mind that even the most competent and dedicated presidents (even those who look and act like the Muppet Eagle) have moments of uncertainty and (dare I say the "f" word?) *fear* teaches that a spouse who is dedicated solely to the president is an invaluable resource.

The mastery of all of these lessons and many others enables the spouse to keep the president sane when all of the gravity of the educational universe is pushing him to the edge of sensibility. The mastery of these lessons is a continuing act of love, lavished on someone who, given the demands which the college places on him, will probably not have the time, the attention, or the energy to fully communicate his appreciation.

The breadth and complexity of learning which a college president's spouse can master are nicely demonstrated by Muriel Beadle, the wife of University of Chicago President George W. Beadle. George Beadle served as university president from 1961 to 1968.

During those tempestuous times all of the social etiquette which had traditionally held institutions of higher education together disappeared. Prior to the mid part of the twentieth century, college education had been reserved for the wealthy or those who were willing to take great financial risks to try to join the wealthy. Student apathy was a given. A working knowledge of Emily Post was required if one were to be accepted as a full-fledged member of a college community. Muriel Beadle was a product of this social milieu and had little experience which would prepare her for urban campus life during the 1960s.

Muriel served as a traditional presidential spouse during the Viet Nam war and the assassinations of Martin Luther King and Robert Kennedy. These upheavals were made all the more challenging because of the University of Chicago's location, south of downtown Chicago and bordered by very poor neighborhoods and neighborhoods which were being elbowed into being very poor. It is hard to think of a more difficult environment for a college, its president, and its president's spouse. Although Muriel did not single-handedly save the University of Chicago or the city itself from these trying times, both were very much the better for her having been there.

Muriel Beadle had all of the interests and talents which one would expect of a presidential spouse of that era. She learned how to run a large house and to entertain well. She was a willing participant in development work and volunteered in the community. Her efforts to improve and preserve the neighborhoods surrounding the university were legendary. Her work in the neighborhoods is still celebrated on the University of

Chicago website. Her focus was not limited to purely residential issues. She understood that diverse neighborhoods survive only if there is commercial life to sustain the neighborhood concept. She worked to create and sustain local commercial enterprises and helped to diffuse old hostilities and to correct planning mistakes. She helped in the preservation of a community of artists.

Also, her understanding of relationships within the university was most impressive. She could be both humorous and insightful, as when she described the provost as "the man who tries to develop at the university those programs which the president in his off-campus speeches says it already has."[101] She continued that if the president was the "Shepherd of the university," then the provost was the "Shepherd's crook."[102] At the same time she well understood that the job of the president was essentially a lonely one and that the president needed colleagues who would be both honest and supportive. She knew that disagreements between the president and provost would necessarily occur, but that those disagreements must never escape the door of the president's office. The argument having been concluded and a decision made, it was the provost's job to make the president's decision manifest on the campus.

She also had a keen understanding of student attitudes and behaviors at a time when most people in

---

[101] Muriel Beadle, *Where Has All the Ivy Gone?* (Garden City, N.Y.: Doubleday, 1972), pp. 101–102 (Beadle was quoting Shannon McLure, former Provost of the University of Massachusetts).

[102] Ibid.

her circumstances simply wrote off college students'
behaviors as the products of sex and drugs. When she
became aware that the university was having a difficult
time appointing students to an honorary society, she
spoke with students, in an attempt to understand their
reluctance to receive what had, in the past, been
considered an honor. She learned that the ethical sense
of the students ran contrary to a process whereby
administration was making discriminations among and
between students in offering these awards. The students
had a sense of democracy which dictated that all of the
stakeholders in the university should have input on such
decisions. Muriel knew that soon enough these same
students would be working for organizations whose
goals could be advanced only by selecting the best
employees. There would be no participatory democracy
in that arena. She also knew enough not to argue with
students on the basis of her experience—an experience
which was not shared by them.[103]

Neither was she naïve about the motivations and
tactics of some students. She told about events occurring
on the University of Chicago campus during World War
I when the university chaplain thanked God for the
congregation's ability to hate the Germans. She then
analogized to some contemporary student leaders who
were demanding that the university promote political
positions of their choosing. Muriel knew that the
obligation of the university was to provide a forum in
which all opinion holders could express themselves. It
was not the university's job to celebrate one ideology

---

[103] Ibid., pp. 166–167.

over another. The crucible of public opinion would take over from there.

She also had a very firm grip on some historical anomalies and financial imperatives which make a college so hard to manage. In her book, *Where Has All the Ivy Gone?*, she discusses the long history of faculty seeing administration as a support entity whose job it is to make sure the teachers are free to teach; some administrators viewing faculty as line employees who can and should be "supervised"; and students believing that both faculty and administration exist to serve their needs—the good ones and the other ones.

> Universities began, in the middle ages, as a conglomeration of Masters around whom groups of students clustered. Only as increasing numbers of students wished to hear the great men lecture did it become necessary to have some kind of administrative apparatus. Someone had to rent the lecture hall; someone had to answer inquiries from aspiring students.
>
> The Masters could have done this themselves, but early on they discovered that if they hired someone to do the clerical work for them they would have more time for research and teaching ... What has evolved is two institutions in one; a businesslike organization that manages the university but does not set policy for the academic side; and the academic side, which determines its own destiny, thank you, but requires the services of the bureaucracy to handle the details. And that's why universities are so hard to govern. You have on the one hand a group of people who are accustomed to the hierarchical relationships of business corporations and consider the administrators to be the holders of *line* jobs in the organization; and on the other hand you have a group of people who consider those self-same administrators to be the holders of *staff* jobs.[104]

---

[104]Ibid., pp. 161 and 163.

Then add to this mixture board members who are largely drawn from business backgrounds and by whom the freedom which the faculty enjoys is viewed as near anarchy, and add further the opinions and judgments of the community within which the university exists, and you end up with a situation very rich in potential for grievous and seemingly insoluble misunderstanding.

Muriel Beadle was a highly scholarly and articulate person who understood all of this and more. She could cogently discuss matters of genetics, institutional governance, student affairs, academic personnel, trustee responsibility (as well as the care and feeding of trustees), morality/ethics, colleagueship, and community relations. I have no doubt that she was equally informed on matters of resources and the allocation of the same. She was not, however, unique in her understanding of the academy. Get current presidential spouses off topics dealing with entertainment and under-appreciation and most will demonstrate institutional savvy which is extensive and deep.

So if, as I suggest, presidential spouses are better off restraining themselves from active participation in the affairs of their spouse's colleges, what is the good of all that knowledge she's "got hold of"? Higher education governing boards are usually made up of successful business and professional persons. Most colleges throw in a faculty trustee, perhaps a staff trustee, and occasionally a student trustee. There are good reasons for all of these choices. Having a student trustee may provide a more direct channel for the communication of student concerns to the board and of board concerns to the students. In any event the appointment of a student trustee disarms the activists' argument that students are not represented at the policy-making level of the college. The same can be said for the appointment of faculty and staff trustees.

Business and professional trustees are also good choices. Frequently they are alumni. Appointment of an alumnus/a to the board sends the message that dear old Alma Mater does not forget her children (or a least a few of them). Businesspersons are also knowledgeable in matters of money acquisition and money management. Their expertise in this regard has been developed in conjunction with the acquisition and management of their own fortunes—a portion of which fortunes is often the unstated quid pro quo for board membership. A few other trustees may be appointed because of their connections with academia generally. These appointees lend an aura of scholarly wisdom to the board.

By and large, presidential spouses with five years of experience know as much or more about the policies and practices of a college than most sitting trustees. Having 85 percent of board members providing expertise in money acquisition and management and offering themselves as development targets is a pretty good higher education practice. However, having 5 percent of that same board providing expertise in the policy, politics, and culture of colleges in general is not bad practice either. It is here that all of that knowledge "she's got hold of" has its greatest value.

Muriel Beadle would have been a great college trustee. Obviously, a presidential spouse could not—should not—will not—serve as a board member at the college where her spouse is president. The idea that a spouse might serve as a board member at the college where her husband is the president is about as loopy as hiring the president's spouse to a paid position at the same college. A presidential spouse, likewise, could not serve as a board member of any college which was, in any significant manner, competitive with the president's institution. However, I believe that she could serve as a trustee of any noncompetitive college to the significant advantage of both colleges. It is very common for presidential spouses to serve on nonprofit boards in their home communities. There is no cogent reason to deprive the higher education community of this considerable resource.

However, some spouses (like some members of the general public), no matter what their experience or acquired knowledge, are not suitable as trustees. Any board of trustees is principally a policy-making body. It is not a super-president. Anyone who has served on boards of trustees has experienced the trustee who thinks he should direct or second-guess every decision of administration. Such a trustee substitutes himself for the administration which the board hired to make just those decisions. Such trustees divert the attention and sap the energy of the board. They are at best tedious and at worst destructive. It is hard for a board to effect policy moving forward the mission statement of the college when the discussion keeps returning to the color scheme of the student center or the record of the football team.

Does the degree of a spouse's involvement in the day-to-day business of a college relate to her suitability as a trustee of another college? My preliminary hypothesis is that the more intimately a presidential spouse is involved in the day-to-day business of the college which her spouse leads, the greater the risk that she would feel the need to superintend the administration of the college for which she is proposed to serve as a trustee. How difficult would it be for the spouse who, in reaction to the one-time use of yellow plastic glasses, completely rewrote the job descriptions of college employees in many departments, to limit her board participation to the cerebral contemplation of policy matters?

I am sure that many involved spouses are capable of reframing their attentions and thereby functioning as competent and effective trustees. Nonetheless, I think it more likely that a spouse who maintains a career or a life independent of day-to-day decision-making at her spouse's college would be a safer trustee prospect. On the other hand, I am familiar with a very small number of presidential spouses who are so self- or career-absorbed that they have virtually no knowledge of important higher education issues affecting the colleges their spouses serve or colleges in general. These folks would certainly be self-eliminating as trustee prospects. If they have no knowledge of or interest in their spouse's college, they will be extremely unlikely to have an interest in another college.

Presidential spouses, be they involved or otherwise, are very knowledgeable about the missions, policies, practices, and personnel of their respective colleges— and other colleges as well. Trustee-appointing authorities would be well advised to consider tapping this largely untapped resource.

David A. Williams

CONCLUSION

So what should all of the stakeholders in the academy do when it comes to the president's spouse? I count the board, the president, the faculty/staff, and the spouse as the primary stakeholders.

All responsibility for colleges and universities is vested in Boards of Directors or Trustees or Overseers. Not only does the buck stop at the board, responsibility for starting the conversation about presidents' spouses' roles starts there, too. Boards should make time to discuss the issue of the role of the president's spouse and to consider the historical, practical, legal, and ethical problems which that role (as generally constituted) creates. With rare exceptions boards should not expect, ask for, or demand services from the president's spouse. They should make it crystal clear to all presidential candidates that spouses will not be expected to work for the college. They should create policies which prohibit the hiring of the president's spouse by the college except in an extremely limited set of circumstances. They should introduce the spouse to the college community and the broader community in which the college is located, making it clear that times are changing and that she should not expect the same old model of the president's wife.

They should facilitate the spouse's connecting with these communities and thereafter just allow her to be herself. They should provide the president with funds which allow him to hire unrelated people to do the work of the college which the spouse has traditionally done.

Much of what I have written was based on my personal experiences. I have written in praise of the two boards which chose my wife to be their president. One was a system board which had responsibility for five public colleges. Individual campuses did not have individual boards. Because of this arrangement and the traditions of the system, the spouses of the various presidents pretty much defined their own roles on campus. Spouses who wanted to be involved were involved. Those who preferred to follow more private roles were allowed to do so. The second board had responsibility for one private college. Again, because of its experiences and traditions, the president's spouse was pretty much free to define her/his role.

In both instances, I was protected in my declarations of noninvolvement by the boards' neutrality on the subject. However, I did not have confidence in their neutrality until long after my wife became president. At the time I made my declarations (during the search process), I made them with considerable anxiety and doubt. If other candidates' spouses were pledging their troths to serve as college ambassadors while I was pledging my troth to my wife, was I putting the kiss of death on her in the search process? I hope that all boards will take the time to examine issues relating to the president's spouse and make their decisions available to all future presidential candidates.

For boards, there remain the questions of how to deal with current, campus-active spouses. These folks came to be where they are because of the long-standing traditions and practices of the colleges they serve. They should be allowed to continue in their current roles for so long as their spouse-presidents hold office. New practices should begin with new presidents.

Faculty and staff should just "let her be." At many colleges, the volunteer services provided by presidential spouses are quickly taken and just as quickly criticized. I have always held a low opinion of those who demand something for nothing and then criticize the something.

Faculty and staff are the standard-bearers of tradition. Their role demands that they critically evaluate the traditions they protect. Prompted by the board, they too should examine the problems which the traditional role of the president's spouse creates for all constituencies of the college. At the end of a fair airing of these issues, I am confident that faculty and staff will discover that they can get along very nicely without supervision by the president's spouse. Absent this kind of board-influenced behavior modification, formal educational programming and/or policy implementation will be required to make these changes known and effective.

All presidential candidates should suck it up and tell search committees that they wish to be considered on their own merits—not on the merits or demerits of their spouses. Such declarations level the playing field for candidates who, for a wide variety of reasons, do not have spouses. In this regard, search firms and committees have a responsibility to educate boards so that they evaluate candidates on their own merits— alone. Presidents should insist that their budgets include funds to pay regular college employees to do the work which has traditionally been done by the spouse.

Spouses should have candid discussions with their spouse/candidates about what the prospective college may and may not expect. Both spouses should be clear and direct in their contacts with search committees in articulating what the president's spouse will and will not do for the college. In particular the spouses should reach an understanding that the college is but an incidental beneficiary of agreements between the spouses and that activities which may benefit the college are secondary to the spouse's preferred activities.

Once the president is hired, the spouse should (figuratively) tie herself to the mast and stuff her ears with beeswax. Eventually, the siren sounds of those who would lure her into discontent will fade. From the president's selection forward, the important relationship will be between "him" (the president) and "her" (the spouse), not "her" (the spouse) and "it" (the college).

The spouse should do her own thing, whether that is neurosurgery, homemaking, performance art, or volunteering. However, volunteering is best done away from the college. There are many worthy causes—and volunteering for most of them should not create problems with the board, the faculty, the staff, or the community. Volunteering at the college sets the spouse on the slippery slope which often leads to institutional expectations, criticism, and discontent.

When boards, presidents, and spouses confuse the spouse's role with a job, there is a problem. Both jobs and roles are found on the highway known as "Work." Jobs, however, are found at the intersection of "Work" and "Compensation." Tangible things are found at that intersection. Roles, on the other hand, are found at the intersection of "Work" and "Creativity." It is here that the intangibles are found—love, friendship, and support. There is no doubt that supporting a college president is work in the sense that it involves considerable effort. However, it is the creative and interpersonal component of that act of supporting which distinguishes that activity from a job. To fill the role of a college president's spouse effectively, the spouse must have her own creative self, substantially independent of the institution which the president serves.

Wherever the intersections of "Work," "Compensation," and "Creativity" are brought together in close proximity on a college campus, other roads are sure to intersect, causing major traffic problems. They include "Faculty Road," "Boardway," "Administration Alley," "Alumni Avenue," "Staff Street," and "Students' Way." If a job description is used as a metaphor for a car, truck, or SUV, everyone working at the college has a vehicle. The only pedestrian in this maelstrom is the president's spouse: She has no job description—or, if she has one, it will not be considered legitimate because the job she has is not one which she got as the result of open, fair competition. This distinguishes her from everyone else on the staff/faculty. There are no traffic lights at this crazy intersection. No matter how quick, agile, intelligent, or strong that spouse is, cars, trucks, and SUVs are faster and heavier. It is only by blind luck or Providence or a lot of planning and resolve that the spouse is going to get across these streets and though this intersection without serious injury.

The intersection needs a traffic engineer who will separate the major highways, moving the intersection of "Work" and "Creativity" off campus. Surely there can be a broad street running from this intersection to the president's house and a narrow alley leading to the campus. The latter might be called "Volunteering Alley." But it should be very narrow—permitting very little traffic. The former might be called "Support

Street" and should have access limited to the spouse and the president. Such an arrangement would protect the spouse, while providing the president with what he needs and the campus what it deserves—a lot of creativity and a very little volunteering.

No one was born a presidential spouse. We all came into this role because of a series of circumstances largely beyond our control. Our situation arose because of our *spouses' talents and achievements.* Some of us contributed to the demonstration of those talents. Just as surely, some of us detracted from such a demonstration. It was largely a matter of chance that we ended up as presidential spouses. In this case, Chance does not confer authority.

But Chance need not define happiness or the lack of it, either. We each have a life to live, regardless of the title, power, and influence of our spouse. We need to live our lives with both love and support for our spouses and with clear respect for ourselves.

A spouse who believes that the institution is taking advantage of her or that it is demonstrating less respect than she deserves is carrying the infectious disease of "Discontent." Discontent spreads easily in small spaces. In the lives of college presidents and their spouses, tightness of time equates with smallness of space. Everything is pushed together by the demands of the calendar. In this environment, a spouse with a serious case of Discontent will affect her spouse. Even if the president does not come down with Discontent, he will be distracted from his duties as he attempts to nurse his spouse back to a state of neutrality. If the spouse's Discontent is chronic, it must inevitably spread to the president with predictable consequences for the college, the president, and the spouse.

Immunization for Discontent is best acquired by rediscovering one's own life and living that life well. There is a wide and wonderful world out there, beyond the ivied walls and spiked gates. All presidential spouses used to live there. Many of the happiest ones still do.

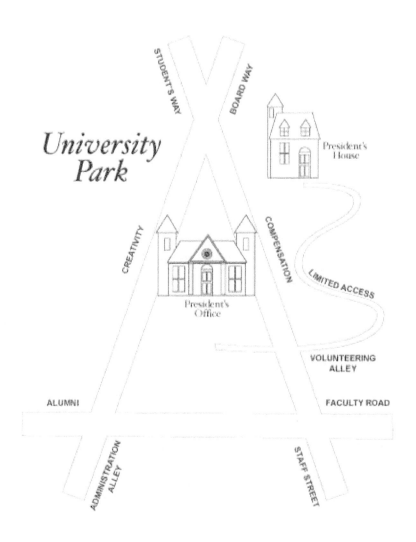

University
Park

STUDENT'S WAY

BOARD WAY

President's
House

CREATIVITY

COMPENSATION

LIMITED ACCESS

President's
Office

VOLUNTEERING
ALLEY

ALUMNI

FACULTY ROAD

ADMINISTRATION
ALLEY

STAFF STREET

Appendix A

CONSTANCE BUMGARNER GEE
Vanderbilt University
211 Kirkland Hall
Nashville, TN 37240
(615) 322-5207

Current Appointment
May 2000-Present
Vanderbilt University
Nashville, TN
Associate Professor of Public Policy and Education, Peabody
College
I have taught *Public Policy, the Arts, and Arts Education* for the
Department of Leadership, Policy, and Organizations and an
introductory public policy course (HOD 2100) for the Human
and Organizational Development Department. My primary
research focus is on the effects and consequences of public
policy on the quality, content, and accessibility of K-12 arts
education and the affects of advocacy on public perceptions of
the purposes and merits of school-based arts instruction. I have
served as an executive editor for *Arts Education Policy Review*
since 1997, and serve also on the board of directors for the Frist
Center for the Visual Arts, and on the advisory board of
Vanderbilt's Curb Center for Art, Enterprise, and Public Policy.

Education
1988-93
The Pennsylvania State University
University Park, Pennsylvania
Ph.D. Art Education
Area of emphasis: Policy analysis and program evaluation
Dissertation Topic: *Artists in the Classrooms: An Analysis of the
Arts in Education Program of the National Endowment for the
Arts.*

1977-79
Pratt Institute
Brooklyn, New York
<u>MFA</u> (highest honors) Painting and Sculpture

1971-76
East Carolina University
Greenville, North Carolina
<u>BFA</u> Painting and Design

Previous Professional Experience
January 1998-May 2000
Brown University
Providence, RI
Assistant Professor of Education and Public Policy
Faculty responsibilities included teaching the course, *Public Policy, the Arts, and Arts Education*; supervision of independent studies; and undergraduate student advisement. Served as a council member of the Rhode Island Philharmonic, Trinity Repertory Company, and WaterFire.

September 1993-December 1997
The Ohio State University
Columbus, Ohio
<u>Director, Arts Policy and Administration Program</u>
<u>Assistant Professor of Art Education</u>
Directed all aspects of the Arts Policy and Administration graduate degree program including curriculum development; thesis advisement for doctoral and master's candidates; internship placement and supervision; and student recruitment. Taught the courses AE 670-*Public Policy and the Arts*; AE 671 – *Community Arts Services;* AE 673 –*Issues Across the Arts*; and a thesis research and writing seminar. Supervised independent graduate study courses, and developed and organized the 1995 Barnett Arts and Public Policy Symposium, and three Barnett Lecture Series programs (1994-1996). Served as a board member for BalletMet Columbus, the Columbus Symphony Orchestra, and the Capital Area Humane Society.

March-November 1991
South Carolina Arts Commission
Columbia, South Carolina
<u>Evaluator/Consultant</u>

Co-conducted an evaluation of a statewide arts education curricular reform initiative (the Arts in Basic Education Curricula Project) sponsored by the South Carolina Arts Commission and South Carolina Department of Education. Researched and analyzed the beliefs and practices of numerous curriculum consultants, district fine arts supervisors, school principals, arts specialists, and classroom teachers with regard to their participation in individual ABC projects. Evaluated the South Carolina Department of Education's arts education curricular frameworks in relation to the ABC legislation.

1988-1991
The Pennsylvania State University
University Park, Pennsylvania
Teaching Assistant, School of Visual Arts
Taught *Concepts and Creations in the Visual Arts and 2-D Design*; assisted in the instruction of *Studio Instructional Methods for the Elementary and Secondary Schools.*

1983-1988
Pratt Institute
Brooklyn, New York
Director, Pratt National Talent Search
Responsible for the planning, development, implementation, and promotion of a $1.5 million scholarship program (annual operation budget $400,00) aimed at recruiting the highest caliber of students in all areas of visual arts, design, and architecture to Pratt Institute. Build a nationwide program support-base among art education administrators, secondary teachers, and professional art education and architecture organizations.

Honors
- Outstanding Educator Honoree, Peabody College, Vanderbilt University, 2000
- The Pennsylvania State University Graduate School Summer Research Fellowship, 1992
- The Getty Center for Education in the Arts Doctoral Dissertation Fellowship, 1991
- Ford Foundation Graduate Fellowship for Artistic Excellence, 1978

Current Professional Associations and Memberships
- *Arts Education Policy Review* (Executive Editor)
- Curb Center for Art, Enterprise, and Public Policy (Advisory Board)
- Frist Center for the Visual Arts (Board of Directors)
- American Association of Museums
- Americans for the Arts
- Council for Policy Studies in Art Education
- International Society for Education through Art
- National Art Education Association

Selected Publications
"Arts Education Advocacy That Works," accepted for publication in *Arts Education Policy Review*, May/June 2007

"Valuing the Arts on Their Own Terms" (Ceci n'est pas une pipe.)," accepted for publication in *Arts Education Policy Review*, March/April 2007

"Spirit, Mind, and Body: Arts Education the Redeemer,: in *Handbook of Research and Policy in Art Education*, E. Eisner and M. Day [EDS.]. (Techbooks) 2004. (Reprinted in *Arts Education Policy Review*, March/April 2004.)

Uncritical Pronouncements Build Critical Links for Federal Arts Bureaucracy," *Arts Education Policy Review*, January/February 2003.

"The 'Use and Abuse' of Arts Advocacy and Its Consequences for Music Education," in *The New Handbook of Research on Music Teaching and Learning*, R. Colwell and C. Richardson [Eds.]. (Oxford University Press) 2002.

"The Perils and Parables of Research on Research," *Arts Education Policy Review*, May/June 2001.

"I Can See Clearly Now: Possible Sequelae of the Reviewing Education and the Arts Project (REAP)," *Beyond The Soundbite: Arts Education and Academic Outcomes* (The Getty Center) 2001.

"Symposium on Arts Education in the 21st Century," Parts 1 and 2 (Ed.), *Arts Education Policy Review*, November/December 2000 and January/February 2001.

"For You Dear — Anything! (Remembering and Returning to First Principles)," Part 2, *Arts Education Policy Review*, May/June 1999.

"The Arts Education for a Lifetime of Wonder," *Educational Leadership*, November 1997. Coauthor. (Titled "Arts Education for Life and Work," this special supplement of *Educational Leadership* combined the proceedings from the Getty Education Institute for the Arts' 1997 national conference, "Educating for the Workplace through the Arts," with contributions from invited guest authors.)

"Four More Years — So What?" *Arts Education Policy Review*, July/August 1997. (An analysis of Congressional dispositions toward the National Endowment for the Arts during the second term of the Clinton Administration.)

"Somewhere over the Rainbow: Dreaming an Arts and Education Community Partnership," *Arts Education Policy Review*, May/June 1997.

"The Religion of Art and Art of Righteousness," *Arts Education Policy Review*, January/February 1996.

"Artists in the Classrooms: The Impact and Consequences of the National Endowment for the Arts' Artist Residency Program on K-12 Arts Education," Part 2, *Arts Education Policy Review*, March/April 1994.

"Artists in the Classrooms: The Impact and Consequences of the National Endowment for the Arts' Artist Residency Program on K-12 Arts Education," Part 1, *Arts Education Policy Review*, January/February 1994

Invited Presentations

"The Future of Art Music: Advocacy that Works," keynote address for the National Association of Schools of Music's annual conference, 13 October 2006.

"Valuing the Arts on Their Own Terms?" keynote address for the National Association of Schools of Art and Design's annual conference, April 2002.

"Strategic Options for Theatre in Higher Education," keynote address of the National Association of Schools of Theatre's annual conference April 2002.

"For Your Dear — Anything! Omnipotence, Omnipresence, and Servitude ' through the Arts'," The Council for Policy Studies in Art Education, National Art Education Association Conference, March 1998; Social Theory, Politics and the Arts Conference, Philadelphia, October, 1998.

"Definitions, Visions, and Purposes of Arts Education," Providence Journal/Brown University Conference on The Arts in America, March 1998.

"Four More Years, So What?", The Council for Policy Studies in Art Education, National Art Education Association Conference, March 1997.

"Rethinking Arts and Education Partnerships: Facing up to and Moving beyond Inter-arts Self-interest," Indiana Arts Symposium XIV, Indiana University, 4 November 1995.

"The Perilous State of Federal Arts Funding: Practical Solutions for Recovery," The Columbus Metropolitan Club, July 1995.

"Arts Education/Arts in Education: What Price Partnerships?" National Art Education Association Conference, April 1995.

"Generating and Renewing Positive Public Values for the Visual Arts," keynote address for the National Association of Schools of Art and Design's annual conference, October 1994.

"Competing Interests and Conflicting Practices: The Character and Significance of Federal Funding for Arts Education," National Art Education Association Conference, April 1994.

DISCLAIMER

Portions of the contents of this book relate to legal concepts. The inclusion of this type of material is intended for informational and educational purposes only. It is _not offered as, nor is it intended to be taken or used as, legal advice_. The laws of many jurisdictions vary significantly. If legal advice is desired, it should be obtained from a competent lawyer licensed to practice (and practicing) in the particular jurisdiction involved. The author specifically disclaims any guarantee or warranty (expresses or implied) relating to the local or general accuracy or usability of any of the contents of this book for legal purposes; and further, the author does not represent that legal materials included in this book are current or complete. Nothing in this book shall be construed to create an attorney/client relationship between the author and any other person.

Appendix B

STATE OF CONFUSION

SUPERIOR COURT COUNTY OF REGRET

DOCKET# 112-09

GEORGE KNOT AND GERRI KNOT, Plaintiffs

VS.

NORTHEAST SOUTHWEST COLLEGE, SHERMAN
STALWART, BOARD CHAIR, AND ALL OTHER MEMBERS
OF THE BOARD OF TRUSTEES OF SAID NORTHEAST
SOUTHWESTCOLLEGE ON JANUARY 15, 2007, Defendants

COMPLAINT

NOW COME George Knot and Gerri Knot, by and through their
attorneys, and make the following complaint:

1. Plaintiff George Knot (hereinafter "George") is a resident of the
State of Confusion and was a candidate for the office of President
of Defendant Northeast Southwest College at Regret. At all
relevant times, Plaintiff Gerri Knot (hereinafter "Gerri") was the
wife of Plaintiff George Knot.

2. Defendant Northeast Southwest College (hereinafter "The
College") is a public college chartered and operated by the State of
Confusion at Regret.

3. Defendant Sherman Stalwart (hereinafter "Stalwart") was, at all
relevant times, the Chairman of the Board of Trustees of said
Northeast Southwest College.

4. Joined as parties to this action are all members of the said Board
of Trustees serving as of January 15, 2007 (hereinafter "the board").

5. During September 2006, The College caused an advertisement to
be published in The Chronicle of Higher Education advising of a

vacancy in the office of President of the College. That advertisement is attached hereto and made a part hereof as "Exhibit A."

6. As a result of that advertisement, Plaintiff George was nominated for the presidency of The College by an academic colleague.

7. At the time of the nomination, George was employed as provost of the University of Contemplation and resided with Gerri at Hobbs, in the State of Clarity. Clarity is a state which is located approximately 1000 miles from Regret, Confusion.

8. Following his nomination, George provided The College with a Curriculum Vitae and letter of inquiry.

9. Shortly thereafter, George was advised that The College had a continuing interest in his candidacy. He was requested to appear for an interview at the Holiday Inn at the Regret Airport.

10. George responded that he would appear for the interview on condition that his interest in the presidency be kept confidential in the initial stages of the search.

11. The College assented to this demand and scheduled the interview.

12. On or about November 15, 2006, George met with representatives of the search committee at the Airport Holiday Inn at Regret.

13. Shortly after that meeting, George was again contacted by the search committee and requested to appear for an interview on the campus of The College.

14. In the course of this conversation the search committee representative advised that if George was married, his wife was also

invited to see the campus and enjoy some time with members of the college community.

15. On December 5, 2006, George and Gerri met with Stalwart and other representatives of the search committee in private sessions and with board members and their spouses at private social events.

16. In addition, Gerri was given a tour of the president's house by board members and met with Tina Tradition, wife of outgoing President Dr. Trevor Tradition.

17. In the course of that tour, Gerri asked her guides what expectations The College had for the president's spouse.

18. Gerri was advised that although there were no formal requirements of the president's spouse, Mrs. Tradition had been very active in campus beautification, community relations, and regular entertainment of both campus- and community-based women's groups.

19. A board member then asked Gerri what her plans were for supporting the mission of The College if George were appointed President.

20. Gerri advised that she was a neurosurgeon with a very active practice in Hobbs. She also advised that she would visit Regret regularly but could not provide the level of service to The College which Mrs. Tradition had provided.

21. On January 15, 2007, George was advised that he was no longer under active consideration for the post of President of The College.

22. On January 16, 2007, Stalwart made a public statement that The College had appointed one Dr. Square Root as the new President. Present at the announcement were Dr. Root; Dr. Root's

wife, Cube Root; Dr. Tradition; and Dr. Tradition's wife, Tina Tradition.

23. Shortly thereafter, George received a confidential communication from a participant in the final search process, stating that George's candidacy was terminated after a board discussion of Gerri's "unwillingness" to be present on the campus in the manner in which Tina Tradition had been.

24. Since Dr. Root assumed the presidency of The College, his wife, Cube, has continued Tina Tradition's work on campus beautification, community relations, and regular entertainment of both campus- and community-based women's groups.

25. Chapter 24 of Title 8-A of the Revised Statutes of Confusion provides: "No person shall be deprived of any employment opportunity on the basis of . . . marital status."

26. Both the Constitution of the State of Confusion and the United States Constitution provide that no person shall be deprived of Due Process of Law or the Equal Protection of the Laws by a state.

27. Upon information and belief, the decision to eliminate George from the candidate pool was based, in part, upon his marital status and in part upon the refusal of his wife to provide services to The College and her refusal to provide these services without compensation.

28. On January 13, 2007, an article appeared in The College student newspaper stating the names of the candidates for the presidency, including George's. Upon information and belief, this information was provided to the student newspaper by a member of the Board of Trustees.

29. As a result of the release of this information, George has been requested to leave his position at the University of Contemplation.

30. As a direct and proximate result of the foregoing acts and omissions of the Defendants, Plaintiffs have suffered the following damages:

A. George has lost his employment at the University of Contemplation with resulting economic losses which cannot be computed with certainty at this time;

B. George has lost standing in the higher education community which will affect his earning power in the future;

C. George has suffered mental anguish and has been held up to ridicule in the higher education community;

D. Gerri has suffered mental anguish which has affected her ability to perform delicate neurosurgery, resulting in substantial economic and noneconomic damages, neither of which can be quantified at this time;

E. Both Plaintiffs had suffered further noneconomic damages.

WHEREFORE, Plaintiffs demand judgment against all Defendants, jointly and severally, in the minimum amount of One Million Dollars per Plaintiff together with appropriate punitive and exemplary damages, attorneys' fees, costs, interest or damages in lieu of interest, and such other and further damages as the Court may deem proper,

Dated: March 15, 2009

Gimmie, Moore & Moore
33 1/3 Contingency Drive
Regret, Confusion

Appendix C

SUPERIOR COURT

COUNTY OF REGRET DOCKET# 666-06

CUBE ROOT AND SQUARE ROOT, Plaintiffs

VS.

NORTHEAST SOUTHWEST COLLEGE, SHERMAN
STALWART, BOARD CHAIR, AND ALL OTHER MEMBERS
OF THE BOARD OF TRUSTEES OF SAID NORTHEAST
SOUTHWEST COLLEGE ON JANUARY 15, 2007, Defendants

COMPLAINT

NOW COME Cube Root and Square Root, by and through their
attorneys, and make the following complaint:

1. Plaintiffs are residents of Regret, Confusion.

2. At all relevant times, Plaintiff Cube Root was the wife of
Plaintiff Dr. Square Root, former President of Northeast Southwest
College at Confusion.

3. Defendant Northeast Southwest College (hereinafter "The
College") is a public college chartered and operated by the State of
Confusion at Regret.

4. Defendant Sherman Stalwart (hereinafter "Stalwart") was, at all
relevant times, the Chairman of the Board of Trustees of said
Northeast Southwest College.

5. Joined as parties to this action are all members of said Board of Trustees serving from September 1, 2006 to date (hereinafter "the board").

6. Dr. Square Root was named President of Northeast Southwest College in January 2007, following an approximately three month search process.

7. Following September 1, 2006, and in the course of that search, Plaintiff Cube Root was informally interviewed by a number of Trustees and other agents of The College.

8. During the course of these interviews, Plaintiff Cube Root asked what expectations the board had of her as "presidential spouse."

9. Plaintiff Cube Root was advised that there were no formal expectations, but that her predecessor presidential spouse, Tina Tradition, had been active in campus beautification, community relations, and regular entertainment of both campus- and community-based women's groups.

10. Shortly after Plaintiff Cube Root's husband, Square Root, assumed the presidency of The College, the Secretary to the Board of Trustees presented Plaintiff Cube Root with a calendar of events at which her attendance was expected. The calendar was the one Tina Tradition would have followed had Dr. Tradition remained in the presidency.

11. The list was very extensive and committed Plaintiff Cube Root to a significantly heavier schedule than she had been led to believe Mrs. Tradition had followed.

12. Although Plaintiff Cube Root tried to keep the schedule provided by the Secretary to the board, it was impossible for her to keep it.

13. Plaintiff Cube Root repeatedly requested the Board Secretary to reduce the number and frequency of required appearances.

14. Eventually, Plaintiff Cube Root's health was affected and she was required to seek medical treatments and counseling.

15. As a direct and proximate result of The College's imposition of this unanticipated schedule, Plaintiff Cube Root became physically and psychologically ill.

16. By reason of the foregoing, Plaintiff Cube Root was not able to allocate sufficient time to her children, one of whom is the subject of a proceeding in Confusion Juvenile Court and another of whom is now incarcerated in Kiddie Correctional Center in Faroff, Regret.

17. Although both children were in good standing, and on the Honor Roll at their previous school, the situation at Regret caused them to become unmanageable and delinquent.

18. After two years of trying to accommodate the schedule provided by the Board Secretary, Plaintiff Cube Root advised that she would not serve The College further and that she was demanding payment for her previously rendered services.

19. As a direct and proximate result of Plaintiff Cube Root's refusal to continue performing services without compensation, Square Root was terminated from his position as President of The College by the Board of Trustees and Stalwart.

20. By reason of this unlawful act by the board, its Chairman, and The College, Plaintiff Square Root has become extremely depressed, causing him to seek medical treatment for both physical and psychological disorders caused by the Defendants' acts and omissions.

21. These events have permanently and irreparably damaged the consortium of both Plaintiffs.

22. Fair Labor Standards and minimum wage statutes of both the United States and the State of Regret require payment by an employer for services rendered by employees and further provide for punitive sanctions for employers who fail to comply with these laws.

WHEREFORE Plaintiffs demand full and fair compensation for:

A. Violation of fair labor standards statutes

B. Violation of minimum wage statutes

C. Intentional infliction of mental and emotional anguish

D. Personal injury, including loss of consortium

E. Other damages as yet unknown

F. Punitive and exemplary damages

G. Attorneys' fees

H. Damages in lieu of interest

I. Costs

J. Other and further appropriate relief.

Dated: April 1, 2012

_____

Want, Mohr, Money, Attorneys
100 Opportunity Lane
Regret, Confusion

Appendix D

UNIVERSITY OF VERMONT AND STATE AGRICULTURAL COLLEGE

BOARD OF TRUSTEES

POLICY ON PRESIDENTIAL SPOUSE OR PARTNER SERVICES

On behalf of the University, the Board welcomes participation by a President's spouse or partner ("partner") in University activities. A partner is not, however, obligated or expected to participate in such endeavors.

If a partner is seeking *employment* with the University, the same policies and procedures that govern other UVM job-seekers apply.

If a partner wishes to offer ongoing *volunteer* services to the University, the procedures below apply.

PARTNER VOLUNTEER SERVICES

At an appropriate time during the process of recruiting a president, the University shall, in writing, provide the candidate(s) with a copy of this policy. The University shall not, however, ask candidates about their (marital or) partner status.

A partner who wishes to offer volunteer services must contact the Vice President for Executive Operations, who will in turn contact the appropriate University official(s).

1 The official(s) will then meet with the partner about prospects for a suitable assignment in view of the interests, qualifications and experience of the partner. The official(s) shall obtain the approval of the Board Chair before offering a volunteer appointment to the partner. A final volunteer appointment letter must describe the nature and extent of any proposed services, including his or her reporting line, and be signed by the partner and the appropriate official(s), including the Board Chair.

Due to his or her status as a volunteer, the partner is not, and shall not be, authorized to enter into negotiations or contracts on behalf of the University. In addition, the partner shall not have supervisory authority over University employees or the right to direct the actions of a University employee in any way. Thus, University employees who are assigned to assist the partner in his or her performance of volunteer work shall be supervised by, and report to, their department head or next-level supervisor.

The officials must minimally include the senior-most person responsible for the activity, operations or program, such as a Vice President.

The officials must minimally include the senior-most person responsible for the activity, operations or program, such as a Vice President.

The University will provide the same insurance coverage otherwise maintained for volunteers to cover the activities of a partner while he or she is engaged in volunteer services assignment. The University shall also cover or reimburse the business travel and entertainment expenses of the partner in accordance with otherwise applicable University policies.

The Board Chair shall meet at least once annually with the partner and the appropriate officials to discuss the ongoing suitability of the volunteer assignments and any adjustments to the assignment that the partner or the officials wish to request. The partner is free to withdraw from his or her volunteer role with reasonable notice to the responsible officials and the Board Chair. Any decision to decline further volunteer services from the partner shall be made by the Board Chair.

To carry out the volunteer duties assumed, the partner may opt for any and all of the following:

●University ID

●University Email Account

●Business Cards

•Parking Permit

The Board Chair must approve any other consideration including equipment purchases, in advance and in writing.

Adopted by: Board of Trustees – October 22, 2011

Made in the USA
Middletown, DE
06 October 2021

49382903R00126